Win Your Partner Back After A Break Up?

How I Harnessed the Law of Attraction to Rekindle My Relationship (And Transformed My Finances, Weight, Health and Social Life Along the Way)

by Louisa Jackson

"Happy relationships depend not on finding the right person but on being the right person"
- Eric Butterworth

CONTENTS

INTRODUCTION

"Those that go searching for love only make manifest their own lovelessness, and the loveless never find love, only the loving find love, and they never have to seek for it"

- D.H. Lawrence

If your relationship has come to an end and you long, desperately, to reunite with your partner - this book is for you. Perhaps you're still with your partner but they're losing interest or pulling away - this book is also for you.

A relationship break up may be one of the most challenging and painful experiences you'll ever face. However, it doesn't always mean the end of the relationship and it certainly doesn't destine you to a lonely and loveless future. In fact, a break up can often be an incredible turning point.

Of course, not all relationships can be saved, and I want to stress this firmly before we begin - I'm not here to give you false hope. Nor am I here to advise on whether you *should* return to your partner. If they were abusive in any way, you'll know already that it's unwise to revisit this type of relationship. If they were unfaithful, only you can decide whether to return.

Some relationships can't be saved and may not be worthy of saving. However, there are those that definitely can, and should, be saved. Given the right inner conditions, broken relationships can - *and do* - heal.

If there is a chance of rekindling your relationship, this book will help you to optimise that chance. This is about magnetizing you for love and bringing a new energy into your relationship.

If you really take on board these principles, I promise you'll achieve at least one - *(and possibly all three!)* - of these outcomes:

- *you'll rekindle your relationship with your partner*
- *you'll attract a new partner*
- *you'll learn how to be happy with, or without, a partner*

I've had my heart broken more times than I care to remember over the years. In my desperation, I read every self-help book I could find. I even spent five long years studying Psychology at University. However, it wasn't until my early forties, during a period of deep emotional crisis, that I felt compelled to learn more about what we now call the 'Law of Attraction'. This led me to delve further into quantum physics and ancient spiritual laws - two very different fields which, perhaps surprisingly, seem to point to the same underlying principles. Almost overnight, my view of the world turned upside down and, after more than two decades of heartache, I finally understood the mistakes I'd been making. Life hasn't been the same since.

It is my hope that the material in this book will spare you some of the heartache I went through. However, this isn't a quick-fix guide. Some commitment and practice is needed. This is a new way of 'being' which will radiate out into all areas of your life. We'll be looking at what's going on *inside* you, rather than on the outer circumstances of your life - for when you transform your inner world, you'll find that your outer world transforms in equal measure. As we'll see later, this isn't merely a spiritual concept but is backed up by quantum physics principles.

The techniques I'll be discussing put an end to my long-term struggle with depression, crippling shyness, bulimia, weight and health issues, financial lack, as well as the cycle of toxic and dysfunctional relationships which I kept repeating over and over. At the very least, you'll learn what *real* happiness is, and how to cultivate it. After all, it's happiness that you're really seeking in your quest to reunite with your partner.

As you'll soon see, learning how to be happy is a vital step in repairing a broken relationship, or in attracting a new and healthy one into your life. You may even find after practicing these techniques that you no longer want, or need, your partner to return.

You may notice some repetition throughout the book and this is intended. Repetition is an essential part of reinforcing new beliefs so that they take root in your subconscious.

I'll use the term 'partner', rather than 'ex-partner', throughout because we don't yet know what the future holds for your relationship. The term 'partner' refers to a girlfriend, boyfriend, wife, husband or lover.

Whether you want to save a long-term marriage or a short-term romance, the same formula applies. It makes no difference if you're male, female, young, old, gay or straight. This is a formula I've used to create a life where I have everything I want, including a loving relationship which was successfully rekindled after applying these principles. Hopefully, it's a formula you'll use forever and one which will slowly - or perhaps quite quickly - bring positive changes to *all* areas of your life.

All names have been changed.

1: First Steps

"Your happiness equates to your capacity to love.
And conversely, all your misery equates to
your need to be loved."

- Lester Levenson

Before we begin the *real* work, we need to stop any behaviours which could be jeopardising the rekindling of your relationship. Sometimes these first steps, alone, can be enough to reignite a relationship. I've certainly experienced this myself and seen it happen with other couples.

1. Behaviours Which Will Repel Your Partner

Even the most level-headed person can behave irrationally during a break up, so don't be ashamed if you've lost control of your emotions. However, if you're engaging in any of the following, I advise you to stop:

- *Begging your partner to take you back*
- *Analysing and discussing your relationship with your partner*
- *Bombarding your partner with texts, emails or phone calls*
- *Declaring your undying love*

- *Trying to please your partner*
- *Giving gifts to your partner*
- *Criticising your partner*
- *Blaming your partner or expressing anger towards them*
- *Stalking, harassing or blackmailing your partner*
- *Acting depressed or seeking sympathy*
- *Trying to make your partner feel guilty*
- *Crying in front of your partner*
- *Expressing jealousy*
- *Giving your partner reasons why they should take you back*
- *Throwing tantrums or being hysterical in front of your partner*
- *Threatening suicide or any other extreme actions*

I've been guilty of most of the above in the past, and it only served to push my partner further away. Underneath these behaviours is fear, neediness, anger and desperation. As we'll be discovering later, you will *never* be a match to love as long as you're radiating these emotions.

2. Surrender to the Break Up

> *"Sometimes letting things go is an act of far greater power than defending or hanging on."*
> - Eckhart Tolle

This next step is also extremely important. It involves the process of accepting and surrendering to the breakdown of your relationship. This, on its own, can sometimes turn things around - even where a partner is seeking a divorce, or has met someone else.

Try to let go of powerful yearnings to pull your partner back. This may seem illogical and very challenging if your entire focus has been on desperately trying to save the relationship. Paradoxically, you have much *more* chance of saving it by giving up on it, than by clinging on to it desperately.

Imagine your partner is a dove that you're releasing into the air. If they want to come back to you, they will do so of their own accord - you cannot influence their feelings. Fear of losing someone can make us hold on tightly. Loosen your grip and they're more likely to return.

If the idea of letting go causes fear, I want to reassure you that immense power comes from non-resistance. As Carl Jung said:

"What you resist, not only persists but will grow in size."

In other words, what you push against you strengthen. Strongly resisting a break up often ensures it remains a break up for good. Letting go, and surrendering to what's happened, is perhaps the most powerful course of action you can take during a relationship breakdown - and I'll explain the science behind this later.

If you still have contact with your partner, and it feels appropriate, it can help to quickly and calmly convey to them that you now accept and agree with the break up. You may feel a very long way from accepting what's happened. However, as you read on, this should begin to change. The more you surrender and let go, the more you'll start to radiate a new and very different energy.

If you've not yet broken up but your partner has suggested a break up, separation or divorce, then gracefully agree with and accept their decision, *without* resistance. Similarly, if your partner is pulling away or seems disinterested, simply allow them to pull away without trying to pull them back. We'll return to the important subject of letting go in the chapters that follow.

3. Cease All Contact

The next important step to take, if you haven't done so already, is to cease all contact with your partner for the time being. This includes emails, text messages and phone calls. This step, like the last, has the power to bring about change, so it's important to stick with this for as long as you can.

This can require great self-discipline. However, now is the time to repair those aspects of yourself which have contributed to the break up, and this is what we'll be addressing.

If you share children with your partner, or still live or work together, you'll no doubt have to maintain some contact. In this instance, simply back off as much as you can, keep communication to a minimum, and keep conversations as upbeat and polite as possible.

If you haven't broken up with your partner but your relationship is in trouble, I still recommend taking time apart to practice the techniques we'll be discussing.

When I say cease contact for the time being, this time period will be different for everyone. In my experience, the longer you take the better. Try to let go of such concerns - this aspect is out of your control. You have essential work to do on yourself now, so the longer you're apart the more progress you'll make.

2: The Spiritual and Quantum Physics Principles Which Changed My Life

"If you want to find the secrets of the universe,
think in terms of energy, frequency and vibration"
- Nikola Tesla

If you're familiar with Rhonda Byrne's *The Secret,* you'll know about your thoughts creating your reality, and like attracting like - what we now call the 'Law of Attraction'. The Law of Attraction isn't a new concept at all - we see references to it in many ancient religions and philosophies. It also underpins the 'New Thought Movement' of the nineteenth century from which classics like Napoleon Hill's *Think & Grow Rich* emerged.

I come from a science-oriented family who fiercely rejected, and often ridiculed, all religious and spiritual concepts. This went back several generations. I now believe this hard scientific approach to life was behind the depression which blighted both sides of my family.

Amongst my parents, grandparents and great grandparents there was a great deal of unhappiness, depression and marital conflict. I was following firmly in their footsteps - until I hit the crisis point which prompted the intense period of study I mentioned earlier.

When I first heard of the 'Law of Attraction', I dismissed it as New Age nonsense. My Psychology degree, after all, had never mentioned such a concept. However, the more I learnt about quantum physics, the more I realized there was truth in what spiritual gurus have been telling us for centuries. Now I had the hard science I needed to take on some of the religious and spiritual principles so absent from my upbringing.

This brought dramatic improvements to all areas of my life, particularly my love life. It seemed I'd been operating with a faulty, back-to-front, view of the world - one that's deeply ingrained in our Western culture today. This, I believe, was at the root of all my heartache.

If you want to change your relationship situation, and improve *all* areas of your life, it's essential to understand the fundamental nature of reality. Without this basic understanding, your life is likely to be full of challenges and unnecessary suffering. That's why, in a moment, I'll outline - as simply as I can - some extraordinary quantum physics concepts which, if they're new to you, should radically alter the way you look at the world. First, though, let's look at some of the spiritual principles which have profoundly changed my life.

Four Spiritual Principles Which Changed My Life

Here are the four life-changing spiritual concepts which I've been able to take on, thanks to the field of quantum physics:

- the concept of 'God' or a 'Higher Power'
- the 'thoughts create your reality' principle
- the 'like attracts like' principle
- the 'Let Go and Let God' principle

For most of my life, I was utterly opposed to the concept of 'God'. However, the more I read about what physicists call the 'Quantum Field', the more the notion of 'God' or a 'Higher Power' made absolute sense.

Whether you call it 'God', a 'Higher Power, 'the Divine', 'Source', 'Spirit', 'the Unified Field', 'the Field of Infinite Possibilities' or 'the Quantum Field' - these terms seem to be referring to the same thing: a universal intelligence which will assist us if we learn how to tune into it.

Now to the next two principles which underpin the Law of Attraction - 'your thoughts create your reality' and 'like attracts like'. The theory is that your 'inner world' of thoughts and feelings produces a vibration which radiates out into the universe. Your 'outer world' of people, places, events and material things reflects what's going on in your inner world. Circumstances which *resonate* with your inner world show up in your outer world. In a nutshell, you get what you vibrate - or like attracts like.

The Buddha spoke of this same principle several centuries ago:

> *"What you think you become. What you feel you attract.*
> *What you imagine you create"*
> - Buddha

Each of us has our own unique vibration or 'energy signature'. This is what we're broadcasting each day with our thoughts and feelings. If you could tease apart your energy signature, you'd find it's a complex mix of different frequencies - there are, no doubt, some areas of your life you feel good about, and others which cause you stress or unhappiness.

Your romantic life is probably a big emotionally charged subject for you at the moment - that's why you're here - so we'll be learning later how to alter your vibration in this area. Part of this involves the fourth spiritual principle - learning to 'Let Go and Let God' - or simply relaxing and forgetting. This tunes you to a happier and more positive frequency which, in turn, allows happier and more positive outer circumstances to materialise. In essence, if you can learn to vibrate *differently*, you'll become resonant with different life situations, and that includes your romantic life.

Fortunately, quantum physics appears to back up these spiritual concepts, which is helpful if you're a cynical non-spiritual type as I used to be. If you want these principles to work for you, it's *essential* that you believe in them - after all, they underpin your entire existence. That's why I'm going to outline some basic quantum physics concepts to support what we've been discussing. Please bear with me if you're wondering how on earth this relates to rekindling your relationship - all will become clear.

The Mysterious Quantum World

Quantum physics is the study of quantum particles - the tiniest building bricks of life. Literally *everything* - including your body - is composed of these particles so it's very important to know a bit about them. The quantum world shows us that life, as we know it, isn't *at all* what it appears to be.

The following is a vast over-simplification of an extremely complex subject. However, these are the essential points to take on board:

1. Everything Is Energy

> *"What quantum physics teaches us is that everything*
> *we thought was physical is not physical."*
> - Dr Bruce Lipton

Physicists used to think that atoms were solid. We now know that if we zoom deep into an atom, then deeper into a sub-atomic or quantum particle, we find it's composed almost entirely - 99.9999% - of empty space. This empty space is filled with energy.

Essentially, *everything* is energy - your entire body, the chair you're sitting on, this book - it's all energy. This energy is vibrating at different frequencies. That's why a wall looks different to a chair or a flower. Similarly, different emotions and thoughts vibrate at different frequencies - hatred and anger are a different frequency to love and joy.

If everything is energy, why do objects seem solid? The reason you can't pass your hand through a solid object is because the energy within an atom is like a swirling tornado. These tornadoes create a powerful force field which resists opposing forces and makes objects feel solid. However, physical reality is really just a vast sea of vibrating energy.

2. Nothing Becomes Real Until It's Observed

> *"As observers, we are personally involved with the creation of our own reality.*
> *Physicists are being forced to admit that the universe is a 'mental' construction."*
> - Professor Richard Conn Henry

Can our thoughts really create our reality? The ground-breaking 'Double

Slit Experiment' in physics helps us answer this. It shows that when a quantum particle is *observed* by a human, it changes from a wave into a particle. To use physicist Fred Alan Wolf's language, it goes from 'gooey' to 'prickly'. In other words, it turns from something hazy and formless into something fixed and real. This is known in physics as the 'Observer Effect'.

This suggests that our physical reality consists of a fuzzy wave-like potential which only materialises into physical form when we observe or interact with it. Make sure you digest this because it's actually utterly mind-blowing.

It means that your outer reality does not exist separately and independently of you. Your mind is *fundamentally* involved in the creation of your day-to-day experience. You craft this field of fuzzy energy with your thoughts and emotions, causing it to crystallize into the objects, people and events in your outer reality. In other words, the *way* you observe and perceive your life profoundly affects what shows up.

Some physicists go as far to say that without a human being in the picture, there's no material world at all - it's all just a projection of our mind. This is a monumental concept to take on board and one that truly turns our view of the world upside down.

Whether you choose to believe this or not, you can be sure that your outer reality is not as fixed and unchangeable as it appears. It is in fact quite fluid and malleable, giving you *much* more power over your outer circumstances than you probably ever imagined.

The entire universe is, essentially, a vast sea of intelligent vibrating energy. Objects look solid and separate but they're really wave-like and deeply interconnected.

On a quantum level, we literally are 'One'. From this field of infinite possibilities, the events and experiences which *resonate* with your inner world come into existence, while those that don't, remain formless.

3. Quantum Wave Functions

Can quantum physics explain the 'like attracts like' principle? Some physicists believe our thoughts and feelings produce vibrations which ripple out through the universe. These ripples are sometimes called 'Quantum Wave Functions', or 'qwiffs' for short - to use Fred Alan Wolf's language again.

Qwiffs travel faster than the speed of light and are thought to seek out other similar qwiffs. Those vibrating on the *same* frequency combine or 'cohere' together to create your next moment in reality. When you feel happy you emit qwiffs of a different frequency to those when you feel anxious, fearful or heartbroken. This 'like attracts like' principle determines what shows up in your life. It's why you get *more* of what you focus your thoughts, energy and attention upon.

We see something a little similar with sound vibrations. Strike a tuning fork with a frequency of 'A' and hold it next to another fork with a frequency of 'A' and you'll hear the second fork vibrate in *resonance* with the first - what's known as 'sympathetic resonance'.

It would, in fact, be more accurate to call the Law of Attraction, the Law of Resonance. Tune yourself to a different frequency and you become *resonant* with different experiences and circumstances.

4. Spooky Action at a Distance

But that's not all - the quantum world behaves in other extraordinary ways. Quantum particles can exist in two places at once, and they can carry information instantaneously across vast distances.

We also know that when two quantum particles come into contact, they become uniquely connected or 'entangled' with each other. Even if two entangled particles are on opposite sides of the universe, a change to one produces a simultaneous change to the other - what Einstein called 'Spooky Action at a Distance'.

If your body is composed of quantum particles, the peculiar behaviour of the quantum world must *surely* affect your experience in the large-scale human world. Telepathy certainly suggests we're 'entangled' with those we're closest to - family, friends and lovers. There's now a large body of evidence to support the existence of telepathy[1] and many, if not most, people have experienced it in their own life.

Just a few weeks ago, as I was walking home, a song I hadn't heard for many years (*I Only Want to be With You* by Dusty Springfield) suddenly popped into my head and I began singing it happily to myself. When I arrived home, I was astonished to discover that my partner had been playing exactly the same song, at around the same time I'd been singing it - a nice example of telepathy. Evidence, surely, that we're invisibly connected. The more relaxed I am, the more I seem to experience these kinds of synchronicities.

If we're all entangled on a quantum level, this means that even if you're physically separated from your partner, an invisible quantum connection remains. A change in your vibration, for example, may trigger a thought or response in your partner - a bit of 'Spooky Action at a Distance'. This may manifest as a gut feeling or an intuitive hunch. It's like a sixth sense you can tune into if you relax and quieten your mind.

These days, I live my life almost entirely by intuition and instinct. This has brought much greater success and happiness than my old logical and analytical approach.

A New Paradigm

Many physicists avoid discussing how the quantum world impacts our day-to-day life. To talk of anything remotely spiritual could mean losing their academic credibility, or even their job. However, I believe we're in the early stages of a paradigm shift. These new beliefs about reality are slowly seeping into the mainstream, though we know from history that it's likely to take a *long* time to be widely accepted, with lots of resistance along the way.

Fortunately, scientists like John Hagelin, Joe Dispenza, Bruce Lipton, Fred Alan Wolf, Gregg Braden and Amit Goswami are now talking openly about these principles. They all agree that the quantum world *hugely* impacts our daily life. And, of course, it hugely impacts our romantic life. We'll look at precisely how in the next chapter.

3: Are You Living Your Life Back to Front?

"Most people would assume my business success, and the wealth that comes with it, have brought me happiness. But they haven't; in fact it's the reverse. I am successful, wealthy and connected because I am happy"

- Richard Branson

The essential point to grasp, so far, is that it's your vibration which comes *first*. Experiences, events and situations in your outer reality which resonate with that vibration then follow *later*. Make sure you fully digest this critical point.

This is not what we're taught in the Western World and most people are unaware of this fundamental principle. We're taught that our outer reality exists separately and independently of our thoughts and feelings. We live life believing that happiness will come *when* we get the outer conditions just right - only when we find 'true love' can we be truly happy.

In fact, the reverse is true - your outer conditions, and your romantic difficulties, will resolve *only* when you get the inner conditions right. The loving relationship, the fulfilling job, the financial abundance - these are all *side-effects* of cultivating the appropriate inner state. You can see from Richard Branson's quote at the beginning of this chapter that he's very aware of this principle.

It's this faulty back-to-front belief about reality which is at the root of so much suffering. It makes us feel like victims and causes us to blame our outer conditions when things go wrong - our partner, our parents, our childhood, the economy, the government, and so on. It makes us feel powerless and at the mercy of outside forces and apparently random events.

If we feel *unhappy*, we're taught to seek solutions to our problems by taking action to control and change our *outer* circumstances. However, this is like trying to alter the reflection you see in the mirror without *first* altering yourself. And yet, this stress-struggle approach is how most people live *all* the time and it's how I lived for decades.

Our culture applauds hard work and struggle and the 'no pain no gain' ethos is deeply ingrained. We're taught that success takes immense effort and hard work. We learn to push through our pain, face problems head on, swim *against* the current and do jobs we don't enjoy, rather than relaxing, feeling good, forgetting problems, using our intuition, going with the flow and allowing life to unfold naturally.

Trying to Control Your Relationship Brings More Unhappiness

This is why desperately *trying* to control your partner's feelings, *working* at the relationship, or *trying* to make yourself more attractive to them never brings results, if internally you're radiating unhappiness and lack. *Any* action taken from a stressed and unhappy inner state will not bring the result you're seeking. In fact, it'll probably make things worse - like attracts like.

I remember all my desperate and manipulative attempts to win my partner's affections in previous relationships. I tried so hard to be the perfect girlfriend - if I could just lose those extra pounds, change my hairstyle, go to the gym, find some better clothes, *then* he'd love me. I'd also play hard to get, or try to make him jealous, in the hope this would change his feelings.

This kind of *trying* is doomed because it comes from a place of lack and it's about controlling and manipulating what's 'out there'. Action taken from a place of unhappiness simply resonates with, and brings, *more* unhappiness. Without changing your inner state *first*, you'll keep recreating the same old unhappy life - year in, year out.

This stress-struggle approach ensures that you live on a permanent treadmill, battling to change your outer circumstances while inside you feel something's missing - usually a lack of love or money, and very often both at once. No amount of action or effort seems to change your situation and you keep repeating the same old problems, over and over. The end result is often depression and I believe this is why mental health is such a big issue in our Western culture.

This faulty back-to-front belief was at the root of my own depression which began in my teens and continued into my early forties. My depression then became yet another 'problem' for me to battle with and seek solutions for.

Not once in my years of studying Psychology at University did we touch on the spiritual laws we're discussing. Depression, we were taught, was a chemical imbalance in the brain caused by genetics and upbringing, and treatment involved anti-depressants and psychotherapy.

I sought out therapists repeatedly over the years and took anti-depressant medication for two decades, as advised by health professionals. However, this approach never led to me conquering my depression. I became resigned to the fact that, like my father and grandfather, I was someone who 'suffered with depression' and that life would always be a struggle.

I *now* know that my only real problem back then was a lack of awareness of the true nature of reality and the basic laws of the universe. My depression stemmed from a faulty set of beliefs about how the world worked - an educational rather than a genetic problem. It was my chronic struggling, worrying and solution-seeking, and my back-to-front belief system, which was causing all my misery. No one ever told me that happiness must come *before* the happy outer conditions can show up. Nor had I ever been taught what *real* happiness is, or how to cultivate it.

I'd picked up this faulty paradigm from my family, school and the whole culture around me. There was, in fact, nothing innately wrong with me or my brain chemistry. I was already complete and whole - nothing in me needed fixing or changing, other than my faulty belief system.

Once I dropped this back-to-front way of living, and took on the new paradigm we're talking about, my depression resolved, and my outer circumstances and love life started falling into place. You'll hear precisely how my life changed in the next chapter.

Like you, and every other person on the planet, I have an in-built capacity to feel joy, I have my own unique qualities and abilities, and I have the power to create the life I want. We must simply tend carefully, each day, to our inner world of thoughts and feelings and make this our highest priority - *above all else.*

When you stop *trying* to control your outer conditions, 'The Quantum Field', 'God', 'Spirit' - whatever you choose to call this intelligence - will take care of the outer details and guide you to take appropriate action as required.

During my depression years, I had no idea that life could be easy, peaceful, happy, relaxed, financially abundant and full of love. This is how my life is now and there's no therapy or anti-depressants involved. Of course, I still encounter challenges. However, I simply do the inner work and issues usually resolve quite smoothly.

I should stress, however, that you should *never* abandon anti-depressant medication suddenly or without medical advice. It took some commitment and practice before I was able to generate my own internal happiness (we'll be looking at how to do this later). And there are some conditions, such as bipolar disorder and schizophrenia, which often do require long-term medication.

I should also stress that some talking therapies available now can be effective, such as Cognitive Behavioural Therapy with its emphasis on thinking. I experienced the older fashioned therapies which involved dwelling on problems intensely, analysing the past in great detail, and blaming our parents for all our troubles. As we'll soon see, focusing intensely on your problems is a great way to anchor them permanently in your life - you get more of what you focus on - like attracts like.

In the same way, I believe relationship therapy can often, inadvertently, reinforce difficulties. By focusing on problems and discussing them endlessly, couples can end up strengthening those issues by feeding them with more energy.

Sometimes relationship therapists encourage couples to work harder at their relationship, communicate more, schedule 'date nights', spend more time together, be more tactile, and so on and so forth. However, without cultivating a peaceful and happy inner state *first*, none of these outer actions are likely to help. Couples might see more benefit if they stopped talking or thinking about their relationship difficulties and diverted their energy into a new hobby or interest.

Why Wanting and Trying Never Works

> *"As long as the thought of 'not having' remains in your mind, you will continue to not have."*
> - Marilyn Jenett

Now you can see why desperate wanting and trying never works - if you're desperately *wanting* your partner and *trying* to win them back, what are you broadcasting? You're broadcasting that you *do not* have your partner. The Quantum Field simply matches your frequency and you continue to *not have* your partner - like attracts like.

You might want to read that paragraph again as it forms the basis of why most people spend their lives desperately chasing dreams that never materialize, trapped in a never-ending cycle of wanting, seeking and trying.

You've Got to Feel Happy *First*

You might expect a book about rekindling love to be full of advice about outer *action* you can take to fix your relationship. However, the focus here is entirely on changing your inner world - this is an inside job.

The only 'work' you ever have to do is to monitor your thoughts and feelings on a moment-by-moment basis. Master the art of feeling consistently good on the inside, and circumstances will rearrange accordingly on the outside - often in quite magical ways. If action *is* required, it'll flow naturally from that happy inner state. Forcing or trying won't be necessary.

If you don't like the music that's playing on the radio, you tune to a different station. In the same way, if you're tuning into a reality you don't like, you need to retune yourself to a different frequency.

Tuning to a loving, peaceful, relaxed and happy frequency will bring corresponding experiences. When you radiate love, you'll experience more love and you'll no longer resonate with heartache and pain.

Precisely *what* and *who* manifests, and *how* and *when* it manifests, is in the hands of the intelligent forces of the universe. However, whatever does materialise will resonate with your new-found happy state.

As you feel happier, desperate wanting and needing will fall away. You'll still have preferences but the desperation will go. This, ironically, is when the things you used to want so desperately start to show up in your life.

Of course, feeling happy will seem quite impossible if you're currently in the depths of heartache. Don't worry - we'll be learning how to ease your way out this in Chapter 6. First, though, a few more important points to take on board.

You Created Where You're at Now

> *"You are today where your thoughts have brought you; you will*
> *be tomorrow where your thoughts take you."*
> - James Allen

It's important to really grasp that the way you've been focusing your thoughts, energy and attention in the past, has created the outer circumstances you're experiencing today. Making this connection is a vital step in breaking a dysfunctional relationship pattern. Your current relationship situation is the *end result* of all you've been thinking, feeling, believing and expecting for some time.

If you reflect on the months, and probably years, leading up to your current relationship situation, you'll see how your inner world has led to where you're at now. Perhaps you've been depressed, stressed or unhappy for some time. Perhaps you've been focusing intensely and fearfully on where your relationship is going, or whether your partner loves you. Perhaps

21

you've had trust issues with your partner, or you've been scared they might leave you. Perhaps deep down you feel unworthy of love.

This may be your first experience of heartache, or it may be a long series of troubled relationships. Perhaps there have been other areas of your life causing you stress which have contributed to a generally depressed state. Any, or all, of the above will have created what you're going through now.

What you're broadcasting, each moment, determines the quality of all your relationships. It affects how your partner treats you, how friends and family treat you, how your boss treats you, how neighbours treat you, and how complete strangers treat you. It also determines the type of partner you attract and are attracted to. When I was deeply depressed, I was magnetically drawn to those who were equally troubled.

If you're radiating an absence of love, you'll experience an absence of love. If you're radiating pain, stress, neediness, hatred, fear or anger, you'll experience more situations that elicit these emotions. If you believe you're unlucky in love, that will be your experience. If you feel unloved or unlovable, or that love is scarce or hard to find, events and circumstances will arise to confirm this - like attracts like.

This can be a hard pill to swallow. It's tempting to blame your partner for the pain you're experiencing now, and you may feel anger towards them. However, it is you and *only* you who has been focusing your thoughts and feelings in such a way to create your life now.

No one intentionally sets out to feel heartache and pain so there's no point blaming yourself. Blame is the wrong word to use here. You've simply been creating your reality *unconsciously,* but we'll be learning soon how to do this in a more conscious and deliberate way.

Forgiving Your Partner

When you really grasp that you created where you're at now, any anger towards your partner, or anyone else, should soften. Forgiveness then becomes possible. Forgiving your partner is an essential step in healing your relationship. Forgiveness creates a much more loving vibration than anger and blame and makes you resonant with much happier circumstances.

Knowing that you create your reality is actually hugely liberating. It means you're not a victim at the mercy of other people or outside events. You don't ever need to battle with, or try to change or control, what's happening 'out there'. Instead, simply turn inwards to work on your thoughts and feelings and the rest will unfold naturally.

Why Problems Keep Repeating

When we repeatedly observe an unwanted situation, with strong negative emotion, we're going to keep experiencing the same, or similar, scenario.

When an unwanted situation repeats, it usually causes us to focus on it with even *greater* negative emotion. This reinforces the experience more deeply and a repeating pattern begins. Hence, the loop of repeating patterns that so many of us get caught in.

You've probably heard of people who repeatedly end up in relationships with a partner who is unfaithful. I was one of those people. The first time it happened - I talked about it, thought about it, cried over it, obsessed over it and became terrified it'd happen again. Like attracted like and history kept repeating itself. This caused me to focus on the problem even *more* intensely and so it kept happening - either with the same partner, or a new one.

For the same reason, people can get caught in repeating patterns of abusive relationships, depression, loneliness, financial hardship, yo-yo dieting, health problems - and so the list goes on. It also explains those annoying little patterns that keep repeating - the infuriating habits of your own that you can't seem to stop, and the annoying habits of those around you.

By repeatedly focusing on, thinking about, and observing these situations with strong emotion, we keep them firmly fixed in our reality. It can be almost impossible to break these patterns if you're unaware that focusing on what you *don't* want, and desperately *trying* to change the situation, *always* brings *more* of what you don't want.

Why Some People Appear to be 'Lucky'

Fortunately, repeating patterns can be created for the *good* things in life. If we focused consistently on what we *do* want and conjured the accompanying happy feelings, we'd all be living rather wonderful lives.

I used to look with great envy at those 'lucky' people who seemed to have everything I longed for - a loving partner, happy family, big house, well-paid job, confidence, financial security and lots of friends. It all seemed desperately unfair when I was working so hard and trying to be a kind and honest person. It simply confirmed my belief that I was deeply flawed, inferior and just plain unlucky.

I now know that 'lucky' people don't achieve their success through luck - they're simply observing their life differently and broadcasting from a happier frequency. Their abundant outer circumstances simply reflect their abundant inner vibration - and they may be quite unaware that this is why they're 'lucky'.

Clearly, it's easier for 'lucky' people to broadcast from a happy frequency because they're *already* observing pleasing outer conditions. This creates a positive feedback loop which reinforces the happy inner and outer conditions.

This is precisely why *'the rich get richer and the poor get poorer'*. It also explains D.H. Lawrence's quote at the beginning of the book:

> *"Those that go searching for love only make manifest their own lovelessness, and the loveless never find love, only the loving find love, and they never have to seek for it"*

This is why so many people get stuck in depression, lovelessness or poverty - often for life. Here is the great conundrum behind the 'like attracts like' principle - how to *feel* loved and loving when all you can see and feel is the absence of your partner and a lack of love. Somehow, you have to feel better *before* the improved conditions can show up.

Fortunately, you *can* do this, and we'll go into the nitty gritty of this in Chapter 6. It can take a bit of effort at first but once you see a few positives in your outer reality, it becomes easier to sustain a happier frequency. Like launching a rocket into space - it takes lots of energy to blast it up there but once in orbit, momentum keeps it there.

Why Letting Go Often Brings Great Results

We've already mentioned the power of 'Letting Go and Letting God'. Sometimes the 'stress-struggle' approach causes us to hit rock-bottom - we become so depressed and exhausted that we give up. However, this is often a turning point where things start to improve.

When we give up, we stop *trying*, take a break from worrying, relax a little and forget our problems for a while. From this more relaxed frequency, a chink of light can shine through - a realisation may be made, a solution may come, or some other helpful guidance may appear.

When I hit my own deepest rock-bottom many years ago, it prompted a period of giving up. This complete surrender brought a strange relief. It was during this period that a helpful neighbour, I barely knew, posted a spiritual book through my letterbox. This was an entirely new subject for me back then, but it was exactly the guidance I needed to put me on the path to the happy life I have now.

Rather than literally giving up on your life, I encourage you to simply 'let go'. When you give up, you feel defeated but when you let go, you have a 'knowing' that things will work out.

If you knew with *absolute* certainty that everything was going to fall into place, any pain you're experiencing now would probably dissolve instantly. Suffering is a lack of trust in the 'Let Go and Let God' principle. If you trusted this principle, there'd be no suffering - you'd know that all was being taken care of. This trust in a higher intelligence will develop as you do the inner work and as you start to see a few positive changes in your life.

4: How My Life Changed After Applying These Principles

"Experiences are preceded by mind, led by mind, and produced by mind. If one speaks or acts with a pure mind, happiness follows like a shadow that never departs."

- Buddha

I'll now tell you what my life looked like when I hit rock-bottom, many years ago. Later in the chapter, I'll describe how my situation changed - at times miraculously - as I put the principles we've been talking about into practice.

Rock-Bottom

I was 42 years old and I'd not had an unbroken night's sleep since my two year old son was born. I was depressed and exhausted. My partner of eight years - let's call him Michael (my son's father) - who I still desperately loved and wanted to be with, despite our very turbulent relationship, was becoming increasingly distant and detached. He was also endlessly criticizing and finding fault in everything I did. Deep down, I knew he didn't want to be with me anymore.

All my suspicions were confirmed when an attractive young woman appeared on my doorstep, one afternoon, to inform me that she was in love with Michael. It seems they'd

26

been seeing each other for a whole year without me knowing. I was absolutely devastated and my life as a single mother began.

Michael moved out and found a place to live around the corner so he could be close to our son. He took with him the two, much-loved, dogs that we'd shared for many years. Michael's new girlfriend moved in with him straight away. Soon, she was in charge of walking the dogs twice a day. This meant that, four times a day, she passed my front door on her way to, and from, the park. Every time I glanced out of the window she seemed to be there, looking like the cat that got the cream.

Even worse, sometimes I'd spot her hand-in-hand with Michael, heading out for the evening, while I faced another sleepless night with my son. Each sighting felt like a knife through my heart. I became acutely anxious about leaving the house in case I bumped into her. Further deep anguish came for me when Michael insisted on giving his girlfriend access to our son. My mental torment, pain and anger was all-consuming, and I spent every minute of my day ruminating about the injustice and agony of it all. Predictably, like attracted like and things continued to spiral downwards.

Further devastation came when I lost all my precious savings - a five-figure sum - after an impulsive business investment went wrong. Then, my brother suddenly became seriously ill with a brain tumour and I had to support him and my elderly parents at a time when I desperately needed support myself. These are the kind of situations that seem to unfold when we're broadcasting from the lowest rung of the vibrational ladder.

I was completely alone, in a big unfriendly city, with no one to confide in and with no friends or family nearby. I had no money to cover the bills, my son was waking two or three times a night, and I was having to support my brother and parents who were also in crisis. In my heartbroken state, I couldn't seem to make meaningful connections with other mothers in the area or find other children for my son to play with. To make matters worse, the bulimia I'd battled with intermittently since my teens flared up horribly due to the stress I was under. I also experienced a kidney stone at around this time - the physical pain of which seemed to perfectly mirror my emotional agony. My ex-partner was loved-up around the corner and offering me no financial or practical support. Having lost my nest egg, I now faced losing the home that my son and I were so settled in.

I remember one evening, in the pouring rain, crouching on the muddy grass in the garden and sobbing uncontrollably. It was at this very hopeless point in my life that I simply gave up. I could see no other course of action to take. I stayed holed-up indoors for several days and simply surrendered to the chaos that my life had become.

It was during this 'giving up' period that the neighbour I mentioned earlier, posted the spiritual book through my letterbox. I'd never discussed my situation with this neighbour, but she must have detected my anguish from afar. This book triggered a long period of intense study and introspection which lasted five or six years. Fuelled by my overwhelming desire for change, I read literally hundreds of books on quantum physics, spirituality and related subjects.

Slowly but surely, as I experimented with what I was learning, I started to experience brief moments of peace. As I altered my inner world and withdrew my energy and attention from my 'problems', things on the outside started to shift miraculously. I'll tell you in a moment what form that took.

When You Ignore Your Problems, They Tend to Resolve

As we've already discussed, letting go is an *essential* step on the path to resolving your relationship situation. Let's look at this more closely.

After endless experimentation, two fundamental principles became crystal clear to me:

- *When you ignore and let go of your problems, they tend to resolve*
- *You don't need to search for solutions to your problems*

This can be summed up nicely with the religious concept we've already talked about - 'Letting Go and Letting God' - or what Law of Attraction books sometimes call 'allowing'. In other words, stop worrying about your situation, and allow the 'Universe', 'God', a 'Higher Power' (or whatever you choose to call it) to take care of it for you. Know that you're not doing this alone - the intelligent forces of nature will guide you at every step if you relax, let go and act on any intuitive nudges that come your way.

A wave of deep peace came over me the day I really grasped this principle. Suddenly, I realized that all the problems I'd spent decades worrying about, and desperately *trying* to solve, were creations of my own mind. I didn't need to *try* to solve them. This was an enormous Eureka moment.

As a child, I intuitively sensed this principle. I remember urging my mother, who was prone to deep anxiety, that if she just relaxed and let go, everything would fall into place. Sadly, I lost touch with this wisdom and it took several decades of chaos to rediscover it.

Of course, this all sounds very counter-intuitive. Our culture teaches us to confront our problems head on, wrestle with them, and find solutions. When a relationship ends, it's easy to become heartbroken, to obsess over it, analyse it, tell our friends and family about it, and to try to fix it. However, turning *towards* the problem, and focusing on it with intense negative emotion, simply brings more of it and stops us accessing a reality where that issue no longer exists.

The solution is, therefore, to turn *away* from your relationship situation. Starving the problem is a *much* more powerful way of resolving it than desperately trying to fix or change it.

At home, I have a small sealed cardboard box with a slit in the top. If a challenge arises, I write down the issue and an ideal outcome on a bit of paper and post it in my box. I then keep letting go of the subject each time it enters my mind, reminding myself that it's all being taken care of. Recently, I opened my box after several years and was amazed to find that nearly every issue had resolved.

People usually fear that if they let go and stop taking action, they'll lose control of their life. However, this is not the case. I've discovered that often no action at all is needed to resolve a problem. If action *is* required, it's the effortless or inspired variety which brings results.

With practice, it becomes easier to know when to take action, and when not to. For example, I try to avoid interacting with anyone if I'm in a negative mood, as this usually brings more negativity. I've also learnt that confronting someone, head-on, about an issue that's upsetting me often causes the situation to degenerate further. Instead, focusing on my ideal outcome and then letting the issue go, often brings a resolution. When you stop forcing and trying, an intelligence flows through you which can feel quite magical. I believe this natural flow is how everyday life is meant to be.

My Big Emotionally Charged 'Problems'

From my teens until my early forties, I spent most of my waking hours wrestling with the following issues:

- *my turbulent and unsatisfying love life*
- *my inability to maintain a committed loving relationship*
- *acute social anxiety and low self-esteem*
- *chaotic eating habits and chronic anxiety around my weight*
- *unfulfilling and poorly paid employment*
- *financial lack*
- *chronic depression*
- *chronic loneliness*

All of this made for a pretty wretched existence. Some of these issues began in early childhood. By my early forties, the chronic worrying surrounding these subjects, and my constant solution-seeking, was so ingrained it was below my conscious awareness. I knew of no other way of being.

My anxious thoughts played repetitively in the back of my mind, all day long, and they were keeping me well and truly stuck. As long as I continued to broadcast this song, with strong negative emotion, I would never access a reality where these problems didn't exist.

Without realising it, I was making myself a perfect match to more of the same. Just as observing an electron turns it from a 'gooey' wave into a 'prickly' particle, chronically observing our problems solidifies them in our outer world. If I'd learned from an early age to channel the same energy into observing the positives that were *already* in my life, I'm sure things would have turned out quite differently.

As Einstein wisely said: *"you can't solve a problem with the same level of thinking that created it"*. In other words, only when you change the way you think about a problem can you access the solution.

Your 'problems' will no doubt be different to mine. However, your love life is probably an area you've been stoking with lots of negative emotion and energy and that's what we'll be looking to change.

How My Life Changed for the Better

"Be realistic: Plan for a miracle"
- Osho

Returning to my own story - when I really put this 'Let Go and Let God' principle into practice and tended daily to my thoughts and feelings, things began to fall miraculously into place, as follows:

The first welcome shift to occur was with Michael. After a year, he and his girlfriend had an ugly break up and she disappeared from my reality. This brought me immense relief. Michael began spending time with our son again and supporting me. He even suggested we get back together, but I intuitively knew this was the wrong path to take. By this stage, my desperate neediness had greatly diminished. In time, I was able to forgive Michael for everything that had happened, and we've developed a very supportive and positive platonic relationship which continues to this day.

The next shift came when my son, at last, started sleeping soundly through the night. My health and energy levels improved dramatically. Further immense relief came when my brother slowly made a full recovery and he remains in good health today.

My financial situation also transformed in magical ways. When I faced losing my home I worked diligently on my thoughts and beliefs about money. After about six months of cleaning up this area of thought, a very elderly and distant relative got in touch (via my Mother), out of the blue, wanting to meet me for the first time - let's call her Phyllis.

Phyllis was an actress. She'd led a colourful life and I was curious to meet her. She lived a short drive away and we soon became firm friends. Some months after our first meeting, she suddenly announced that she'd made out her Will and was leaving her property to me when she died - a very valuable property I should add. I was absolutely stunned. I'd never once mentioned my financial difficulties to Phyllis. This was the kind of 'manifestation' I'd read about in Law of Attraction books but never dreamt could possibly happen to me. Now I had tangible proof that my inner work was bringing outer results. The 'Universe' really did seem to be taking care of me.

I should add that Phyllis is still very much alive at the time of writing this, and long may that continue. However, her extraordinary gesture gave me a huge feeling of abundance and firmly cemented my trust in these spiritual principles. This feeling of abundance seemed to unleash further financial miracles.

Shortly after Phyllis' gesture, a close friend of my father's died and left him a significant sum of money. My father decided to give the money to me - and not my brother. Again, I'd never mentioned my financial crisis to any family members. My Scottish father has never been known for his generosity, so this gesture was very unusual and out of character. Michael also started helping me financially for the first time. Financial assistance just kept coming and, against all the odds, I was able to stay in my beloved home.

My newfound trust gave me the courage to quit my unfulfilling, low-paid, job and to pursue my own creative projects. This was the path I'd always longed to take but had never dared. It was a huge leap of faith, but it paid off and I'm now more financially secure than ever, and my 'work' no longer feels like work.

As the years passed, my deeply ingrained problems resolved, along with a host of minor issues. My social confidence and social life improved dramatically. Some of my less functional friendships simply fell away. These were people I'd clung to during my depression years - we were now no longer resonant. In time, I made new and more positive friendships. My eating and weight struggles also resolved. Even my chronic asthma dramatically improved after I made changes to my diet and lifestyle, putting an end to decades of daily steroid medication.

After about four years of being happily single, the icing on the cake came when I unexpectedly met my current partner - let's call him John. If my story sounds a bit too good to be true, rest assured, it wasn't all plain sailing. Things with John were wonderful at first but after a year we hit a few road bumps and he ended the relationship. My old trust issues and insecurities resurfaced and caused some conflict.

Fortunately, due to all the inner work I'd already done, this break up was the easiest I'd ever experienced. I did feel sad, but this time I knew the inner work required and I diligently practiced the methods in this book. Mentally I let go of John, making no attempts to contact him, or pull him back.

Soon, I was feeling happier and became engrossed in other areas of my life. I trusted that circumstances would resolve, one way or other, in my best interest. After six months of no contact, John got in touch - out of the blue and of his own accord - and we had a blissful reunion.

I'm certain that working on my inner state is what made me resonant with our happy reconciliation. Had I desperately clung to the relationship, or stayed in deep depression, as

I'd always done in the past, I don't think John and I would have reconnected.

I went on to resolve the trust issues which contributed to our break up (more on this later) using the techniques in Chapter 9. Ten years on, John and I still enjoy a very loving partnership of a kind I've never experienced before.

I should stress that none of this was an overnight transformation. Some issues resolved quickly, while the more deeply rooted ones took several years to resolve, with a few hurdles along the way.

As my mind became more peaceful, I was no longer resonant with my old problems and habits. They simply fell away - often quite unexpectedly and with little planning or action on my part. Solutions often seemed to appear from nowhere when I wasn't consciously seeking them.

Why People Often Fail With the 'Law of Attraction'

> *"If you want anything at all, you can have it,*
> *providing you stop wanting it."*
> - Lester Levenson

If you read any Law of Attraction book, it'll tell you - quite correctly - that if you want to 'manifest' something, you must feel as though you *already* have what you're trying to manifest. Like then attracts like.

Rhonda Byrne's *The Secret* has made various techniques popular, such as vision boards, visualising and positive affirmations. To rekindle your relationship, therefore, you might try to see yourself strolling along the beach, hand-in-hand with your partner in a state of deep bliss, or put a photograph of yourself and your partner on your 'vision board', or repeat some positive affirmations.

Now, there's nothing wrong with these methods and they can be effective if you're trying to manifest a neutral material object like a car. However, these methods often backfire because people start using them during the agony of a break up or financial crisis. As we've already discussed, desperately *wanting* and *trying* to manifest something when you're radiating pain and lack, just brings more pain and lack.

Trying to feel as though you're 'in love' when you've just had your heart broken is virtually impossible. And visualizing your partner simply stirs up painful emotions, making you *more* aware of their absence which, in turn, helps to maintain their absence.

You'll have the same difficulty trying to feel abundant if you're in deep financial crisis - the jump is just too steep. I wouldn't recommend these techniques unless you're *already* feeling happy and peaceful.

Another problem with these methods is that a five minute visualisation, a few affirmations, and some glances at your vision board isn't going to do much if you spend the remaining 95% of your day consumed with negativity. The old thinking that got you into trouble in the first place is still broadcasting in the background, all day long, and your dominant vibration remains unaltered.

This is where many people abandon Law of Attraction principles and remain firmly stuck where they are.

What's the Solution?

How do we apply these spiritual principles to rekindling your relationship?

1. Tackle Pain First

The first vital step is simply to start feeling a little better. This is the focus of Chapter 6, where we'll learn how to deal with painful feelings. Then we'll start to strip away the mental stories which may be keeping you stuck in heartache. This is a bit like reformatting the hard drive of a computer and installing a new operating system.

Repeatedly letting go of thoughts about your partner, reduces the energy invested in the 'problem', paving the way for a resolution - whatever that may be.

2. Trust Universal Intelligence

Handing your relationship issue over to a higher power, or universal intelligence, is another essential step. It's not your job to solve your break up. Your job is to let go of the oars and allow life to unfold naturally.

3. Tune to a Happier Frequency

The ultimate destination - the feeling we're all seeking and one that *really* magnetizes you for love - is a peaceful and loving state which we call 'happiness'. Tackle your pain first and it becomes easier to start accessing this state. This is the focus of Chapters 7 and 8.

As you begin to feel better, the visualising so often recommended in Law of Attraction books will start to happen naturally. This isn't something you should ever force. Just as negative imagery comes naturally to a negative mind, happy thoughts and daydreams are a by-product of a happy mind.

4. Understand What 'Real' Happiness Is

If a happy inner state is the gateway to manifesting love, you *have* to understand precisely what 'happiness' means. If you're deeply *unhappy*, you'll almost certainly have some faulty beliefs about happiness which have contributed the breakdown of your relationship. We'll look at this *very* important subject next.

5: What Is *Real* Happiness?

"Happiness is our natural state. That which prevails
when we reset the computer."
- Francis Lucille

If happiness is the perfect state for rekindling love - and all other good things - we need to know what this elusive state is all about. If only this subject were on the school curriculum, it would save most of us a lifetime of chasing happiness in all the wrong places.

The pursuit of happiness isn't selfish. In fact, it should be your number one priority. Being happy not only changes *your* life but improves the lives of other people. When you're unhappy, you hold yourself back and pollute the worlds of those around you. Yet so few people seem to know what happiness actually is.

The Happiest Man in the World

I've learned a lot from a lovely Frenchman called Matthieu Ricard who's been dubbed 'the happiest man in the world'. In his twenties, Ricard gave up a career in biology to become a Buddhist monk. He developed a great interest in the subject of happiness. With his scientific training, he's been able to back up his theories with real science. In clinical studies, Ricard's brain showed the highest levels of activity ever seen in the area associated with happiness - the left pre-frontal cortex.

Ricard attributes his happiness not only to daily meditation but also to his beliefs and way of perceiving the world. He achieves this blissful state despite being celibate and having few material possessions.

Happiness Is Not the Same as Pleasure

Ricard stresses the fundamental difference between 'pleasure' and 'happiness', and this is the essential point to grasp. Confusing pleasure with happiness is what our culture is based on, and it causes endless suffering.

Pleasure is a fleeting and temporary state - what we feel when we watch a good film, have sex, eat a delicious meal, go on holiday or buy a new car. However, pleasure does *not* bring lasting happiness. Pleasure and happiness are *entirely* different states.

Ricard stresses there's nothing wrong with enjoying pleasurable activities. He gets great pleasure from watching football. You should still enjoy pleasurable activities, as long as you know that these won't make you happy. They're just a complement to your existing happiness - the icing on the cake, rather than the cake itself.

Unhappiness often drives people to seek happiness in eating, shopping, smoking, sex, drugs, gambling or alcohol. These activities, however, only bring a quick pleasurable fix. When the pleasure wears off, we may get the urge to repeat the activity and this can lead to addiction. Chasing pleasure in the belief it'll make you happy, is a recipe for great *unhappiness*.

It's easy to confuse the pleasure of an intense sexual relationship with happiness. When the sparks stop flying, any underlying unhappiness that was there *before* the relationship began will quickly rise to the surface. We then look at our partner and think 'you're not making me happy anymore' when in fact, *we* are the cause of our unhappiness.

For many years, I lived like a desperate 'love junkie', always craving my next relationship fix. When a relationship ended, I'd go through agonising withdrawal symptoms. I was so terrified of being alone that I'd desperately search for a new relationship if I sensed my current partner was losing interest. I'd seek refuge in the arms of the most unsuitable men, believing any relationship was better than being on my own.

Real Happiness Can't be Found in Another Person

Like most people, I grew up believing a romantic partner was my passport to true happiness. Hollywood certainly promotes this fantasy. It's this faulty belief that's at the heart of many – if not all – dysfunctional relationships. If there's one core belief you need to change, it's this one. You do *not* need a partner to feel complete because you are *already* complete.

The potential to feel joy lies *within* you, not outside you. You, and *only* you, create your own happiness. This heavy burden is not one to place on your partner, or anyone or anything. You'll never find lasting happiness 'out there' in any person, circumstance, activity, event or material thing.

It's this mistaken belief about happiness that often prompts people to seek a new relationship when things *appear* to go wrong in their current one. The same feelings of dissatisfaction simply repeat in the next relationship when the honeymoon period wears off – and so the cycle continues.

Being in a romantic relationship can, of course, bring lots of temporary *pleasure* but this isn't real happiness, as we can see from Matthieu Ricard's simple celibate life.

In the same way, the amount of money you have makes little, if any, difference to how happy you are. Studies show that as long as your basic needs are met – a roof over your head, food, warmth and other necessities – making lots of money won't make you any happier[2]. And yet, so many people chase wealth believing it's the key to eternal happiness.

The good news is that happiness isn't something only the lucky or privileged can experience. You don't need to envy people with more money, a bigger house, better looks or a better car than you – these will have brought them temporary pleasure only and *not* lasting happiness. The other wonderful news is that when you stop desperately chasing happiness in your outer reality, all those things you were so desperately chasing - the love, the wealth, the health and so on - are much more likely to materialize.

This means you can stop chasing happiness in the external world, because happiness costs nothing and is achievable regardless of your circumstances. This came as a huge relief to me.

Desperately chasing happiness 'out there' in relationships, activities and material things only left me feeling empty, depressed and exhausted. If you can really grasp this, you're on the road to true inner peace and joy.

It's Not Your Partner's Job to Make You Happy

> *"Relationships don't cause pain and*
> *unhappiness. They bring out the pain and unhappiness*
> *that is already within you."*
> - Eckhart Tolle

Your partner is not the cause of your happiness or your unhappiness – *you* are. Realising this was a huge turning point for me. I'd always placed a heavy burden on my relationships, making my partner responsible for the way I felt. His behavior could plunge me to the depths of despair or lift me to a state of bliss. If he wasn't sufficiently attentive or caring, my mood would plummet. This then triggered arguments where I'd try to get to the bottom of his uncaring behavior.

These attempts to elicit the loving response I craved never worked because I was seeking happiness in the wrong place. I entered all my dysfunctional relationships in a depressed state, believing the relationship would cure my depression. There were moments of great pleasure, but my faulty beliefs about happiness lay unaddressed and my depression remained.

The way your partner responds to you is largely determined by the energy you radiate. If you radiate love, peace and happiness, rather than need and lack, they'll respond in a like manner. Cultivate your own inner happiness and your partner is likely to respond in a more loving and attentive way.

Stop Waiting for Happiness

"It is not uncommon for people to spend their
whole life waiting to start living"
- Eckhart Tolle

Many people spend their entire life waiting to feel happy *when* the right outer conditions show up, while internally they're radiating emptiness and lack. This is certainly how I used to live.

Before I became a mother, I believed that having a baby would make me the happiest woman on earth. I waited for motherhood for a long time, believing this was the missing piece of the jigsaw which was going to solve all my unhappiness forever. I love my son more than anything in the world. However, after the initial euphoria of being a new mother wore off, I quickly returned to my old depressed state. This came as an enormous shock to me - nothing 'out there' it seemed was ever going make me happy.

At the moment, you may be waiting to feel happy *when* you rekindle your relationship. You may argue that reconciling with your partner will bring enormous happiness. You may even feel your whole existence hinges on this event. However, unless you've *already* mastered the art of real happiness, a reconciliation will bring you temporary pleasure only.

Happy circumstances won't make you happy - it's being
happy that creates happy circumstances.

If your happiness depends on having specific outer conditions in place, when those conditions change, as they usually do, you're setting yourself up for great suffering.

The ultimate solution - one which I continue to master - is to cultivate an inner peacefulness *regardless* of what's going on around you. That's when you're truly free. Then, even if you experience loss, there's still an underlying wellbeing that's always close to the surface.

Your Happiness Thermostat

Ricard's studies show that we each have a baseline of happiness which is high in some people, and low in others - a bit like a thermostat that's set to a particular level.

Studies of lottery winners show that after an initial period of elation, one year later, most winners have returned to the baseline emotional state they were in *before* they won the lottery[3] - whether that was happy or unhappy.

So, even after an extreme life event, we usually revert to our default happiness setting, whatever that is. If you were unhappy *before* your relationship began, that unhappiness is likely to return when the honeymoon phase wears off.

Fortunately, you can raise your happiness baseline with the techniques we'll be covering. I have successfully done so, and my improved outer circumstances beautifully reflect my inner transformation.

So What Is *Real* Happiness?

If happiness is not the same as pleasure, and it can't be found 'out there' - what, then, is real happiness?

We often think of happiness as an excited or elated state but it's not realistic, or even desirable, to be excited or elated for any length of time. This isn't real happiness. Real happiness is a peaceful and relaxed state.

Ricard defines happiness as follows:

> *"to be free from constantly ruminating over the past or constantly anticipating the future with hopes and fears, expectations and doubts. It is to be able to remain in the present moment without being disturbed by craving, anger, jealousy, and so forth. It is a state of freedom from mental toxins."*

So, here we have the secret to eternal happiness summed up beautifully in a few sentences.

Babies and young children are in this state most of the time and are naturally joyful as a result. They live in the present moment, with no concern for the past or future - emotions come and go but the happy state is always close at hand.

You were born with this innate capacity for joy. It's still there for the taking - right under your nose - and you don't need to search for it 'out there'.

By adulthood, most of us have lost touch with this state - it's been buried under layers of faulty thinking and conditioning which we've accumulated over the years. It can take some practice to remaster this state. However, the secret to lasting happiness is really very simple.

Your thoughts and beliefs are *not* who you really are. The real 'you' lies *underneath* this mental debris. This happy, spontaneous, side of you will emerge as your mind becomes quieter and more peaceful.

You don't need *anything* to be happy. However, the perfect relationship, house, career, car, social life - should you want those things - are *much* more likely to materialize when you broadcast consistently from a relaxed and happy inner state.

Happiness flourishes if you systematically strip away thoughts that relate to fear, guilt, judging, criticising, envy, greed, pride, impatience, competitiveness, anger, frustration, hatred, obsession, arrogance and jealousy, and instead develop a more loving, relaxed, generous, grateful, kind, patient and compassionate way of looking at the world.

Living in the Here and Now

"The more consciousness you direct into the inner body, the higher its vibrational frequency becomes. At this higher energy level, negativity cannot affect you anymore, and you tend to attract new circumstances that reflect this higher frequency."
- Eckhart Tolle

An *essential* ingredient of happiness is being present in the moment. All our happiest moments are when we are truly present in the here and now. You will only ever find happiness *right* now - where else could you possibly find it? The past and future don't exist, except in our mind. This is the subject of Eckhart Tolle's best-selling book *The Power of Now*.

Tolle was tormented and depressed during his early life and came close to suicide several times. However, one night, aged twenty-nine, he experienced a profound 'inner transformation'. He had the thought: *"I cannot live with myself*'. This thought made him realise there were two parts of himself - the 'I' who cannot live with 'myself'. Suddenly, he detached from the thoughts in his head and *"the suffering self collapsed as if the plug had been pulled out of an inflatable toy"*. Underneath his thoughts, he could sense a presence and aliveness.

After this dramatic shift, Tolle abandoned his academic career and spent the next few years wandering, homeless and unemployed, *"in a state of deep bliss"*. Over time, his outer circumstances changed to reflect this inner bliss - he became a spiritual teacher, found his soulmate and became a best-selling author.

For most of us, this inner shift won't happen overnight. However, it can be a huge turning point just to know that your mind, with all its faulty thoughts and stories, is what's causing you to suffer. When you stand back and watch your thoughts and realise they are not who you really are, happiness *will* follow. The real 'you' lives underneath this mental chatter.

Suffering stems from a loss of connection with the present moment. As Tolle puts it:

"All negativity is caused by denial of the present. Unease, anxiety, tension, stress, worry - all forms of fear - are caused by too much future, and not enough presence."

When we're truly present, we drop our anxieties and problems. In doing so, there's a letting go, and we stop broadcasting negative thoughts and feelings. This moves us to a new and different frequency which, in turn, brings changes to our outer circumstances.

All of my major 'manifestations' have come during periods when I've religiously practiced living in the present moment. Conceiving my son, unexpected financial windfalls, solutions for my asthma and bulimia, and rekindling my current relationship - all came, along with numerous smaller 'miracles', when I focused diligently on being in the present moment and consistently let go of negative thoughts and feelings.

Being present tunes you to a natural flow and intelligence which will guide you, step by step, to a happier life. This is when synchronicities, coincidences and 'out of the blue' events start to happen. These are a sign that you've tuned to a new frequency - nature's way of matching you with circumstances which resonate with this new frequency.

Being present can be extremely challenging during a break up when the mind often becomes intensely agitated. We've all had those moments, when we think to ourselves - *"I can't take this anymore"*.

If you're in this state, stop and look around you - are you comfortable, can you see anything pleasing, what sounds are there, are your problems here with you now, and is there any immediate danger? Usually, 'right now' is absolutely fine. Rarely are there threats in our immediate environment. In other words, it's simply the mind which is making us suffer, rather than what's *actually* happening right now.

The more you fully experience 'now', the more joyful and spontaneous you'll become. As Tolle says, being present creates a protective energy field around you which insulates you from negative circumstances.

A quick way to become present is to feel the energy flowing through your hands or feet as you focus on your breathing. You might want to try this right now for a few minutes.

Alternatively, you can focus on the sights and sounds around you. If you were painting a still life, or landscape, you'd look with great intensity at what you were painting. When you really look around you and listen, it's amazing how you see and hear things that were always there, but you'd been too lost in thought to notice.

Staying present when I eat has helped me recover from the eating disorder I mentioned earlier. I now eat mindfully, rather than mindlessly shovelling food down while thinking about something else.

Your mind will wander off continuously when you first try this but with practice, you'll be able to stay present for longer periods. When I first read Tolle's *The Power of Now*, nearly twenty years ago, I toyed with the idea of having the word 'Now' tattooed on my wrist as a permanent reminder. Back then, my mind was so tormented I found it impossible to stay present for more than a few seconds. However, I returned to Tolle's book years later when I finally realised that the only way out of my misery was to connect with now. That's when life really began to improve.

In the next chapter, we'll start tackling your painful thoughts and feelings so that you can more easily access the power of 'now'.

6: Moving Out of Heartache and Pain

*"The sun is always shining, you need
only remove the clouds."*
- David Hawkins

We've established that your thoughts and feelings determine what shows up in your life. We also know that *real* happiness is a relaxed and peaceful inner state where you're fully present in the moment and free from toxic thoughts. The more you tune to this frequency, the more you resonate with the experience of love, and other pleasing circumstances.

Before you can tune to this state, we must tackle your *unhappiness*. This involves stripping away the mental debris that's built up over the years, especially in the area of relationships. This is like restoring a computer to its factory settings. Remove your faulty programming and you'll uncover your innately joyful nature. This takes practice, so it's worth investing time in this chapter. Once mastered, Chapters 7 and 8 will move you further up the vibrational ladder. First, let's deal with your feelings.

Feeling Your Feelings

Your thoughts generate feelings, and your feelings radiate out from your heart. The human heart generates a powerful electromagnetic field, much stronger than the energy field of the brain. What you're radiating from your heart is what really shapes your outer circumstances, so it's very important to process your feelings properly.

The pain I used to experience after a break up isn't something I'd wish on anyone. Although a distant memory now, I remember feeling real physical pain in my chest, as if my heart was literally breaking. I could barely eat or sleep and getting through the day was agony. If you're in this really crippling phase at the moment, let me reassure you that there is a way out and it may be easier than you think.

Stop *Trying* to Feel Better

Dealing with painful emotions is quite simple - stop *trying* to feel better. If you want a feeling to pass quickly, it's important not to resist it because *"what you resist persists"*. Forcing a smile on your face, or making yourself think positively, will only make your pain more excruciating. Trying desperately to *stop* pain, usually prolongs and deepens it.

If you're around people, it helps to seek solitude so that you can do this properly, and so that others aren't drawn into your emotions. If your pain is intense, allow yourself to rest and, if you can, take a break from daily chores and activities.

Sit quietly and *really* allow yourself to feel your feelings as fully as you can. Surrender and dive into them head first. Focus all your attention on *exactly* where you feel the pain. This is a chance to study the sensations in your body. Redirect your attention *away* from your mind and into your body. If you've never done this before, you may find it an interesting exercise. Where in your body do you feel the emotion - in your face, chest, heart, arms, legs, stomach? Welcome the emotion and feel it as intensely as you can. Take deep breaths and if tears come, allow them.

Feelings tend to dissolve quite quickly if you allow yourself to feel them. Surges of emotion may return through the day, so stay with them if you can. Eventually, calmness will return and your mood will lift. The trick is to catch and observe an emotion just as it forms. This stops it spiralling out of control. With practice, you'll get good at spotting less intense, and more subtle, feelings which come and go throughout the day and are often suppressed.

Don't Throw Wood Onto the Fire

Often our thinking becomes very distorted when we're in pain. Negative thoughts flood in, to fuel and amplify the emotion. This is like throwing wood onto a fire. It adds *another* level of pain to what you're already feeling. Try to catch yourself doing this. Feel your feelings, physically, in their purest form, without attaching sad thoughts and stories, and they should soon dissolve.

I used to spend hours sobbing uncontrollably after a break up. I'd stoke my pain with tragic stories about my situation while listening to melancholy music for hours on end. This would usually go on for weeks, and sometimes months.

It's important to feel your feelings, but you don't have to amplify them. I was simply magnifying my pain unnecessarily and broadcasting it with great intensity. This ensured that the heartache would repeat again in months and years to come, which it most certainly did - like attracts like.

Emotions Are Simply Movements of Energy

> *"All emotions are just movements of energy. Not good. Not bad.*
> *Not painful. Not pleasurable. Not anger or happiness or frustration."*
> - Robert Scheinfeld

From an early age, we're taught to label our feelings as either good or bad. We give them a name like 'happiness', 'sadness', 'anger', 'frustration' or 'jealousy'. However, emotions are simply 'movements of energy', *rather* than something negative or unwanted. Seeing them in this way, reduces their intensity. Simply allow these waves of energy to pass through you, without naming them.

Young children process their feelings in the instant they arise. They don't hold on to them tightly, attach stories, or suppress them, as we do as adults. This allows them to move from extreme distress to elated happiness in an instant. At some point during childhood we lose this wonderful ability to allow feelings to pass quickly through us like waves. With practice, though, you can relearn this skill.

Don't Suppress

It's tempting to push pain down because it's too overwhelming to allow it in. Habits like smoking, drinking alcohol, over-eating, taking drugs, arguing and controlling are often used to avoid painful feelings. However, these are temporary escapes which bring no real relief.

If you have a craving for an undesirable habit - examine and sit with the feeling of craving. Allow it in, and it should soon pass. If it returns later, simply repeat the process. With practice, you may find you've conquered an unwanted habit or addiction.

It's also tempting to suppress negative feelings for fear of 'manifesting' something bad in your life. This was my concern when I first heard about the Law of Attraction. I would force a smile on my face and try to think positive thoughts. However, I will stress this emphatically - you must *feel* your feelings. Once a feeling has arrived, it's real, it's happened, and there's no reversing it. The only logical course of action is to feel it.

Suppressing feelings puts a barrier in front of your natural joyfulness and makes pain more intense. Suppressing over long periods can cause chronic depression.

Allow your feelings to pass through, as they arise, without naming them or attaching stories, and you'll discover a contentedness that's always there in the background, waiting to surface.

Training Your Monkey Mind

> *"If you correct your mind, the rest of*
> *your life will fall into place."*
> - Lao Tzu

Now, let's turn to the root of all human suffering - our thoughts. Just as the heart, liver, kidneys and other organs go about their business continuously, the brain is busy churning out thoughts all day long. These thoughts generate feelings and the resulting vibration shapes your life.

This gives you a powerful incentive to censor your thinking. And yet, so few people practice this. You know what happens if you neglect your body, but are you aware of the consequences of neglecting your mind?

Left to its own devices, the human mind will run wild - what Buddhists call the 'monkey mind' - incessantly chattering and jumping from thought to thought. Training the monkey mind, by becoming aware of our thoughts, is a central practice of Buddhism often known as 'mindfulness'.

Disciplining your monkey mind will, quite simply, change your life. I cannot stress this forcefully enough. It's a fundamental life skill I wish I'd been taught as a child. My own dysfunctional thinking became deeply ingrained from an early age, causing me decades of intense suffering. However, with daily practice, I've completely transformed my mind and life has fallen into place as a result.

From the moment we wake, to the moment we fall asleep at night, we can easily spend around sixteen hours engaged in pointless and repetitive thought. That's about 20,000 to 50,000 thoughts a day. If most of these thoughts are negative, that's a *lot* of negative broadcasting.

This repetitive background noise is what's shaping your life. If you don't like what's showing up, you *have* to pay close attention to this endless stream of thought.

Most thoughts are unnecessary and bear no relation whatsoever to what's *actually* happening to you right now. Some thoughts may be useful - an idea or intuition that arises from a still mind. However, most thoughts are unhelpful distortions of the truth - like static interference on a radio.

It's as if there are two worlds existing in parallel. There's the imaginary world in your head, full of stories about the past and the future. Then there's the sensory world where things are happening *right now* - birds singing, the sound of traffic, bodily sensations, clouds drifting by, and people going about their day.

Look around you now - what can you see and hear? What else are you aware of with your five senses? You'll find that the sensory world of 'right now' is a much happier place to live than the chaos of the mind.

The ultimate goal is to keep your mind as still and peaceful as possible, for as long as possible, and to stay anchored in the present moment. This is about creating as many moments as you can each day - however brief - where you let go of problems and anxieties.

These moments of stillness are when we're happiest and most creative. This is when we 'Let Go and Let God' and allow a higher power or universal intelligence to flow through us. This takes practice, but it's a skill which will completely transform your life - and that includes your romantic life.

Now, here's the good news - if you've been a chronic negative thinker for most of your life, as you let go of negative thoughts by the thousand each day, the positive impact on your outer circumstances is likely to be *more* noticeable than it is for those of a more optimistic nature.

The other good news is that you don't need to totally remove all negative thought to experience change - just a small inner improvement can bring *significant* outer improvements.

Your Break Up Story

> *"The primary cause of unhappiness is never the*
> *situation but your thoughts about it."*
> - Eckhart Tolle

The first thoughts we'll tackle are those relating to your relationship situation. Some people bounce back quickly after a break up, while others stay heartbroken, sometimes for years, unable to move on.

Some sadness is quite natural after a break up but what you don't have to endure is the paralysing heartache I used to be so familiar with - the kind that makes it difficult to function and may even prompt some people to take their own life. Suicide was never an option for me, but I certainly thought about it, often, in my darkest hours.

If you're experiencing this very intense pain, I have some wonderful news:

> *It's not your break up which is causing you pain but the story you*
> *are telling yourself about your break up.*

Please read this again and make sure you fully digest it.

Your break up story is your own unique interpretation of what's happened. Even if you haven't broken up, but your relationship is in trouble, you'll still have a story about your situation. This story is just a collection of thoughts that you're thinking repetitively and believing to be true.

If you've been talking to others about your situation, you'll probably know roughly how this story goes. Alternatively, you may be quite unaware of having such a story. It'll be running silently, and hazily, in the back of your mind - a blurred mix of thoughts, feelings and images. It can take some digging to uproot this story, but it will be there. If there's suffering, there's *always* a story lurking in the background.

If your pain is intense, your break up story will consist of some very faulty thoughts and beliefs. It's these which are triggering your emotional pain, *rather* than the break up itself.

For me, this story was a fairly typical tale of woe which went roughly as follows:

"I'm not good enough. I'll never find love again. I'm unlovable. I'm ugly. Love is hard to find. I can't be happy on my own. I'll never be happy again. My life's a mess. He was 'the One'. Life's not worth living. This pain will never end. Nothing will ever change. He never loved me. He doesn't care. I'm in agony. There's no future for me"

None of these thoughts are facts - they're interpretations, and extremely faulty ones at that. I'd also torture myself with agonising visual images of my partner enjoying himself with another woman, without a single thought for me.

By repeating this tragic story to myself and others, I was broadcasting it with powerful emotion and keeping myself firmly stuck where I was. This ensured that my pattern of heartache and failed relationships kept repeating.

This is a *guaranteed* way to keep an unhappy relationship pattern recurring in your life. It also helps to block a potential reconciliation with your partner. Often, I'd stay stuck in heartbreak for months on end, only to repeat the same situation some time later, either with my most recent partner or a new one. Like kept on attracting like.

Write Your Break Up Story Down

The first step is to write down the thoughts surrounding your relationship situation on one half of a piece of paper. You may have to dig deep to pull out these fleeting thoughts. However, it's well worth investing the time to uproot them. Once written down, draw a line down the middle of your page. Then, on the right-hand side, write down a new list of thoughts which are roughly the opposite of each of those on the left-hand side.

Please note - I'm *not* suggesting you adopt the new thoughts in your right-hand column. You'll encounter great resistance to doing so if you're in a lot of pain because they simply won't be believable at the moment. Later, as your mood lifts, you may be more receptive to these new thoughts.

The point of this exercise is to show that there are an *infinite* number of ways of interpreting your situation. No single interpretation is more correct or valid than any other. The interpretation you choose, determines how the next chapter of your life will unfold. That's why it's *so* important to look closely at these thoughts.

Here's an example of an old and new version of my break up story:

My Old Story	**A New Story**
I'm not good enough	*I'm good enough*
I'll never find love again	*I'll find love again*
I'm unlovable	*I'm lovable*
I'm ugly	*I'm attractive*
Love is hard to find	*Love is everywhere*
I can't be happy on my own	*I can be happy with, or without, a partner*
I'll never be happy again	*Happiness is my natural state*
My life's a mess	*I have much to be thankful for*
He was 'the One'	*There are many potential partners for me*
Life is not worth living	*Life is worth living*
This pain will never end	*I'm starting to feel better*
Nothing will ever change	*Things are starting to change*
He never loved me	*He'll always love me*
He doesn't care	*He still cares*
I'm in agony	*I feel better today*
There's no future for me	*I see a positive future ahead*

I think you'll agree, when you read the new story in the right column, it feels uplifting compared to the devastating story on the left. This new story, had I believed it, would have produced a very different outcome.

Just imagine how you'd feel if you truly believed the new thoughts in your right-hand column. How would friends and family react if you incorporated one or two of these into your conversation?

If you find this exercise difficult, an alternative is to talk your story through with a friend, or therapist, to find new ways of looking at your situation. Therapy and talking can be helpful if it makes you reinterpret what's happened more positively, as long as there's a letting go of the issue afterwards. This changes what you're broadcasting which, in turn, changes what materialises outwardly.

You Can Interpret Your Break Up In *Any* Way You Choose

You can actually interpret your situation in any way you choose. *Everything* we think and say is an interpretation we've conjured in our mind. Change your perception of any situation and you change what shows up. If you can really take this on board, you're on the road to a wonderful new life.

For some people, a break up is a positive and liberating experience. Your break up has this potential too and, it's entirely possible that, one day you may see it this way.

Your Break Up Is Neither Good Nor Bad

> *"Nothing is either good or bad, only thinking makes it so"*
> - William Shakespeare

You don't *have* to attach any interpretation at all to your break up. It may be hard to believe this, but a break up is neither good nor bad - it's a *neutral* event. Of course, a break up can trigger what we call 'sadness' - a movement of energy of a particular frequency. However, it's the mind which chooses whether to amplify this 'sadness' into intense suffering by creating a tragic story.

The human mind is a highly sophisticated interpreting machine. It labels, judges and interprets *everything* - all day long. Just watch it in action. You'll soon see how everyone is interpreting and judging. However, none of these interpretations are true. The only truth lies in what's happening right now - what you can see, hear, smell, taste and touch - all else is a mental concept.

With daily practice, I've learned to observe my interpreting machine from a distance and know that I don't need to buy into its stories. As a result, I now rarely get upset over the small stuff, *or* the big stuff, and my depression is most definitely a thing of the past.

Disabling the Old Story

> *"The moment you start watching the thinker,*
> *a higher level of consciousness becomes activated."*
> - Eckhart Tolle

Once you've examined your break up story, and realised it's just a story, the next step is to catch these thoughts as they flit through your mind.

You don't need to spend every waking hour doing this. Nor do you need to replace your negative thoughts with positive ones - this will happen naturally as your mood lifts. Simply observing these thoughts will slowly reduce their frequency and this is all that's needed. However, the more time you invest in this, the quicker your life will improve.

When you bring these thoughts about your partner and relationship right into your conscious awareness and shine a bright spotlight on them, you halt them in their tracks. Once observed, they tend to dissolve. This is a bit like birdwatching - sit back and wait for the next thought to appear. What variety will it be?

There's no need to fight your thoughts - this should be a gentle activity. Welcome them in and simply watch them pass through. Choosing not to follow, or engage in, them stops them running wild.

Many of your break up thoughts will be wisp-like and below your awareness. They'll flit by silently, but they can still hugely impact your mood. With practice, you'll get good at catching these faint background thoughts. Also watch out for any unpleasant visual imagery that accompanies these thoughts.

As you withdraw energy from your relationship 'problem', the old story will start to wither away. As I mentioned in Chapter 4, when I systematically pruned away my anxious thoughts about money, my financial situation transformed, miraculously, in ways I could never have imagined. In the same way, as you reduce negative thoughts about your relationship situation, you become resonant with something better.

Keep *Feeling* Your Feelings

Observing your thoughts can be challenging during a break up. Thoughts can become obsessive and intrusive and it may be hard to think of anything other than your partner. This mental torment often arises when a negative feeling is trying to surface that you're not allowing. This causes your thinking to distort. Remember to keep feeling your feelings in the way we discussed earlier, *without* feeding them with stories, and your mind should quieten.

Later in the chapter, I'll give a simple but powerful technique to help if your thinking has become very out of control.

Watch Your Words

Not only do we broadcast with our thoughts, but also with the words we speak - this includes written communications such as emails, text messages and social media posts. Like every thought you think, every word you speak or write, sends a ripple out into the Quantum Field which shapes what comes next.

If you need to talk about your relationship with others, keep conversations constructive and focused on what you *do* want, rather than on what you don't want. Endlessly talking about your relationship woes, or complaining about your partner, will keep you stuck where you are.

With practice, conversations will become lighter and more cheerful. Negative and complaining conversations will start to feel repugnant and you'll want to quickly change the subject or walk away.

Weeding Out Other Negative Thoughts

Once your break up thoughts have reduced, you can start stripping away other unhelpful thoughts. You don't need to hunt for these - just wait and watch and see what comes up.

Some of my very limiting thoughts began in childhood and they still surface occasionally. However, I've largely weeded out the worst offenders with lots of intense self-monitoring over the years.

Here are some examples of my old negative thoughts:

- *People don't like me*
- *People find me boring*
- *People think I'm strange*
- *Good things never happen to me*
- *I've suffered a lot in my life*
- *I had a difficult childhood*
- *I suffer with depression*
- *I'm unlucky in love*
- *I'll never be confident*
- *I have to be slim and beautiful to be loved*
- *I have to work hard to achieve success*
- *I've made a mess of my life*

Some of these thoughts seem absurd now. However, they were so deeply ingrained, I barely knew they were there. They were part of what I thought was 'me' and events in my outer reality arose to support them.

Some of these thoughts fuelled my chronic shyness and social anxiety. With careful monitoring, I noticed that before, during, and after every social interaction, I'd have a cascade of negative thoughts and feelings about myself, what I'd said, and what I thought the other person thought of me. These thoughts were so automatic and unconscious, I'd never questioned them. As I worked at pruning them away, my social confidence improved dramatically.

Also watch out for critical, judgmental, paranoid, angry or jealous thoughts. Judging, complaining and criticising is a toxic habit. Whether you think such thoughts privately or verbalise them, they'll lower your mood and bring more things for you to judge, criticise and complain about.

Worrying is also a chronic habit for many people. When you worry, you radiate fear and block the solution to the very thing you're worrying about. Try to catch yourself in the act. Also watch for imaginary arguments and conversations - something I used to engage in a lot.

Carve Out Sections of Time Each Day

As your mind quietens, you'll experience more and more moments of *real* happiness. Daily commitment is needed here - like weeds, negative thoughts will grow back at every opportunity.

The trick is to find brief moments to do your 'birdwatching' - in the shower, on the way to work, while brushing your teeth or waiting in a queue. Or, simply sit down for a few minutes and see what thoughts arise.

It helps to ask this question periodically:

What reality am I creating with my thoughts right now?

In other words, do you *really* want these thoughts to manifest outwardly? Endlessly brooding on a subject will keep it firmly anchored in your life.

Be vigilant at night as you go to sleep, and when you wake in the morning. Negative thinking at these times can affect the quality of your sleep and set the tone for the day ahead.

You're likely to relapse repeatedly to your old thought patterns and this is to be expected. This isn't something to try for a few days. Put your heart and soul into this - make it a commitment for life - and I promise you *will* reap the rewards.

Tackling Persistent Negative Thoughts

Some thoughts can be very repetitive. Again, writing these down can help you to reinterpret a situation.

My mother was diagnosed with breast cancer in her fifties. Thankfully she survived and is still alive and well, over thirty years on. However, as I approached fifty, I began to worry intensely that the same experience would befall me. My anxious thoughts became very persistent and repetitive. I even started imagining lumps in my breast. Everywhere I looked, I'd hear stories about cancer. I then started worrying that all my worrying was making me resonant with the cancer I was so desperately worried about!

When I wrote down all my anxieties and examined them logically, I found new ways to look at the situation. This inspired some action - I started having regular check-ups and made preventative changes to my diet and lifestyle. This allowed me to let go of my anxious thoughts and I've permanently changed my beliefs around this subject.

Happiness Will Shine Through

If you can monitor your thoughts for long enough, and keep returning to the present moment and your five senses, happiness *will* follow. Sunshine will start to break through the clouds periodically.

Happy moments may take you by surprise, often in the most mundane situations - perhaps while shopping, brushing your teeth or washing the dishes. This is *real* happiness because it's not arisen in response to a pleasurable outer experience. You'll feel a spontaneity and aliveness and the real 'you' will start to emerge. This happiness has always been available to you - it's just been buried under layers of faulty thinking.

Pain is Your Teacher

Whenever you feel upset, you can be sure there's a faulty mental story that needs uprooting. Pain is a useful alarm bell - it tells you that your mind has wandered, and you've disconnected from the present moment.

As my mind has quietened, I've become acutely sensitive to the smallest dip in my mood. When your mind is still, it's easy to spot a tiny ripple on the surface. Welcome your pain, for it's nature's way of guiding you back to stillness.

Ho'oponopono

I mentioned earlier a simple, but powerful, technique which can help when your thoughts become very intrusive. This technique can be a lifesaver during stressful times. In fact, I find it useful even when I'm feeling good. It can also help to ease emotional pain.

Ho'oponopono (pronounced ho-o-pono-pono) is an ancient Hawaiian practice for quietening the mind. You can read about this technique in Joe Vitale's fascinating book *Zero Limits*.

Ho'oponopono simply involves repeating a mantra, silently to yourself, as you go about your daily activities. This clears away thoughts and restores your mind to the peaceful state we've been talking about - what Vitale calls 'getting back to zero'. In this 'zero state', guidance and inspiration can flow through you more easily. The clearer your mind, the faster your life will fall into place.

Vitale likens negative thoughts to computer viruses. Repeating your mantra 'cleans' the mind of these viruses. Vitale says he 'cleans' all day long. Your mind will drift off repeatedly - just keep returning to your mantra.

The usual Ho'oponopono mantra is *"I love you, I'm sorry, please forgive me, thank you"*. Vitale explains the significance of this particular mantra in his book, which we won't go into here. Personally, I don't think it matters what your mantra is - as long as it's something fairy neutral or pleasant. I simply repeat a single word, as in transcendental meditation.

Repeating your mantra helps to stop intrusive thoughts about your relationship and helps starve your 'problems' of energy. This has been a vital tool in overcoming my depression and social anxiety. I no longer think the tormenting thoughts that made me depressed and socially anxious.

Sometimes I repeat my mantra out loud when I'm at home alone. This makes it easier to spot when my mind has drifted off. After several years of practicing, my mantra kicks in automatically if I feel stressed. I recommend Vitale's book if you want to go more deeply into the Ho'oponopono method.

Meditation

Meditation is another wonderful route to mental stillness. I find meditating with others is particularly blissful. Meditating in times of emotional turmoil can be challenging but this gets easier as your mood lifts. I will stress, though, that thirty minutes of daily meditation won't have much impact if you let your mind wander off during the rest of the day. Monitoring your thoughts throughout your day - like a form of wakeful meditation - brings even bigger rewards.

Why Repetition Is *So* Important

Scientists used to think the neural pathways in our brain were set in stone by adulthood. However, the field of 'Neuroplasticity' now shows that we form new pathways right up to the day we die. This plasticity means we all have huge potential for change. You really can 'teach an old dog new tricks'.

No one has to be stuck with a tendency towards depression or being unlucky in love. You can change these tendencies by pruning away the underlying faulty thinking. You really can become a happy optimist who's lucky in love - and I offer myself as proof that this is possible.

Watching your thoughts each day, lays down new neural pathways to support this new monitoring habit. There's debate as to how long we need to practice a new skill before it becomes habitual and hardwired. However, studies suggest that *at least* two months is a good starting point[4].

Dedicate at least two months to observing your thoughts and there's a good chance it'll become a permanent habit. Not only will you lay down new neural pathways to support this habit, but the circuitry supporting your old negative thoughts will slowly wither away. Like a well-trodden pathway in the country, if the path is no longer used, it'll grow over and disappear. Similarly, the more you practice being present in the moment, the more habitual and hardwired this habit becomes.

This is why repetition is so important if you want to permanently change your life. Give up too soon and you won't have laid down the necessary circuitry for lasting change, or allowed the old pathways to wither away. However, once the new neural architecture takes root, your outer circumstances *will* change to reflect this.

7: Tuning To A Happier Frequency

"The vast majority of people are born, grow up, struggle, and go through life in misery and failure, not realizing that it would be just as easy to switch over and get exactly what they want out of life, not recognizing that the mind attracts the thing it dwells upon."

- Napoleon Hill

If you've been practicing what we've covered so far, your mood should be lifting. You may even be having brief moments of happiness for no particular reason. If you are, you're making excellent progress. Once you feel consistently better, you can start to reach for feelings further up the scale.

There's no right way of doing this and you may find your own methods - simply pick those which resonate, and practice and repeat. However, I *don't* recommend this chapter if you're still in heartache - the jump will be too steep. Spend more time on the exercises in Chapter 6 until you feel better.

Fortunately, you don't need to feel permanently blissful to see improvements in your life, although this would certainly speed things along. Just a slight upward shift can bring noticeable results.

Remember to keep monitoring your thoughts and allow your feelings to pass through without fuelling them with stories. Keep diverting your attention *away* from the mind and into the present moment and your five senses.

Here are some powerful techniques for maintaining a happy mood:

1. Turn Away from Negatives

> *"Whatever we put our attention on will grow stronger in our life"*
> - Maharishi Yogi

An essential life skill to master is the art of turning your attention *away* from anything upsetting - whether that's in your mind or your surroundings. If you dwell on upsetting things, more upsetting things will come your way.

If you want to change your relationship situation, you have to stop chronically observing the 'problem' and the absence of your partner. This can be difficult to do at first but if your pain is sufficiently intense, you'll summon the discipline to channel into this.

If there are reminders of your partner in your home - perhaps photographs or gifts which make you sad - put them out of sight. Nor does it help to listen to sad music which stirs up painful memories.

This is the greatest challenge in harnessing the 'like attracts like' principle in your favour - how to feel good when all you can see, and feel is the absence of the thing you so desperately want. This is about learning to feel better *before* the outer conditions have improved. This involves protecting your inner state from outside contaminants and not letting outer circumstances dictate how you feel. It's about swiftly changing your focus in the same way you change the TV channel - and you may have to change channels repeatedly during the day.

The happier I've become, the more I'm affected by distressing news stories. For this reason, I avoid the news as much as I can - I literally do change TV channels if something upsetting comes on. However, there was a time when I barely reacted to traumatic headlines because I was *already* so depressed.

My elderly father spends much of his day fixated on the negative news stories around the world. It's no surprise that he's chronically depressed and anxious. If only there was a 'good news' channel instead of the gloomy headlines we're all so accustomed to.

Unless you're going to actively help in the tragedies of the world, getting upset about them only adds to the collective consciousness of fear and negativity. What a different world it would be, if we were all radiating peace and joy.

It also helps to insulate yourself from the negativity of others. If, like me, you have friends, relatives or neighbours prone to pessimism, you'll need to divert negative conversations, or limit your time with these people. I've developed a real distaste for chit chat that involves complaining or criticizing. However, I used to engage in this kind of talk a lot.

You'll no doubt find other pollutants you can avoid. I used to repetitively check myself in the mirror, weigh myself, and scrutinise my finances each day. When I stopped all of this, these particular issues slowly resolved - my weight dropped, I made peace with my reflection and my financial situation transformed.

This may sound like a form of denial. However, this isn't about ignoring an important issue that needs your attention - you should always take action as needed. This is about reducing time spent dwelling on problems so that you don't lower your mood and draw more negativity towards you - ignorance really is bliss.

2. Exaggerate the Positives

As well as turning *away* from the negatives, you can learn to turn *towards* the positives. This means dwelling on any good feelings or events that come your way. I used to be highly skilled at this but with the *negatives* rather than the positives, and this created an endless cycle of unhappy experiences. I'd complain endlessly about a bad experience, have real and imaginary conversations about it, and endlessly ruminate on the subject. However, if you reverse your focus from negative to positive, you'll get caught in a wonderful cycle of positive events.

If you're a parent, this principle can work wonders with your children's behaviour. Focus on the good behaviours, rather than the bad, and you'll experience a well-behaved child.

Here are a couple of ways to exaggerate the positives:

a) Celebrate!

If anything good happens to you - no matter how small - celebrate it with everything you've got. Jump up and down, throw your hands in the air, say *"Thank you!"* out loud, log it in a notebook, tell your friends about it, take photographs, have imaginary conversations about it, and try to hold on to the good feeling for as *long* as possible - even if it's something as trivial as finding a parking space!

Keep broadcasting these celebratory 'qwiffs' and you'll soon experience more to celebrate - a cascade of happy events will follow.

b) Wallow in Your Good Feelings

As well as celebrating, watch out for any good feelings that arise. These may come for no reason, or in response to a thought or an event. No matter how fleeting the feeling is, try to hold on to it for as long as you can. You can then relive these happy moments to tap into the happy feelings again.

If something makes you laugh or smile, dwell on the bodily sensations and extend the feeling for a bit longer. This is like looking for waves to surf - even if you only surf the wave for another ten seconds, this adds up through the day.

As an experiment, I recommend finding something that makes you laugh. There's a wealth of funny material on YouTube - animal videos always work for me. What does a smile feel like? Really focus on the subtle changes in your facial expression and the physical sensations that arise when you feel good.

Another good time for this is in the shower or bath - wallow in, and accentuate, the pleasurable sensation of being in warm water. Regularly immerse yourself in these positive states and you'll reset your happiness thermostat to a whole new level.

3. What Can You Appreciate?

Almost every spiritual or Law of Attraction book I've ever read, stresses the importance of gratitude and appreciation - that's because it works. I credit this practice with turning my life around. I still practice this daily, even if it's just for brief moments.

Here's what Rhonda Byrne, author of *The Secret*, has to say about gratitude:

"I have seen miracles take place in health where there seemed to be no hope. I have seen marriages saved, and broken relationships transform into magnificent relationships. I have seen those in total poverty become prosperous, and I have seen people in depression catapult into joyful and fulfilling lives"

The quickest way out of the darkest hole is to start appreciating, and making peace with, where you're at now.

I recommend buying a notebook just for this purpose. Quickly jot down, each day, *anything* you can appreciate in your life. Start with something small - a smile from a stranger, the sunshine, a good night's sleep, a cup of coffee. Just allow things to pour out without much thought. Don't worry if you repeat the same list each day - you'll soon attract new things to appreciate.

There are probably *many* aspects of your life you take for granted - the roof over your head, friends and family, a warm bed, running water, sanitation, electrical gadgets, a country without war, food to eat, your sight, hearing, arms, legs, mobility, your health and the health of those close to you. Not everyone has these things. You probably have no idea just how lucky you really are.

You can practice appreciation anytime and anywhere. This muscle strengthens with daily practice. As you change the way you see your life, your outer circumstances *will* change to reflect this.

If your attention slips to negative subjects, turn to your notebook and remind yourself of what you've written. If you feel resistant to doing this exercise, as I did initially, begin with one minute of appreciation a day and build on that. Such a *tiny* investment for a potentially huge pay-off.

4. What Does Your Ideal Life Look Like?

Much of our suffering is caused by focusing repeatedly on what we *don't* want - this the best way to create a life that you *don't* want.

If you're upset about a situation, here's an important question to keep asking yourself:

What do I want in this situation?

Imagine your ideal outcome and focus not only on the specific outer details, but on how you'd like to *feel*. Few people spend time imagining their ideal life and that's why so few people are living their ideal life. Remember, you have to conjure the good feelings *before* the outer conditions can show up - like attracts like.

I recommend writing down, in *great* detail, what your ideal life looks like. What does an ideal day look like? I love doing this and always drift off into happy daydreams. Once you've conjured the desired feelings and images, enjoy wallowing in them for a while. Then, simply 'Let Go and Let God'. A few minutes of this each day will bring *much* greater results than any outer action taken from a place of stress and lack.

I don't recommend focusing on your relationship situation for this exercise in case it stirs up painful emotions. Other areas of your life are just as important such as platonic relationships, hobbies, interests or projects. Focusing on these areas shifts your attention *away* from your love life, and we know already that doing so is what allows your romantic situation to change.

With practice and repetition, your subconscious will slowly start to believe that you're *already* living your ideal life and it'll set about guiding you in that direction. This is where intuitive nudges come into play. Act on these nudges and they're likely to bear fruit.

It's important not to lose sight of your ideal vision. I keep my written account with me always. If my mind wanders onto unwanted things, I look at my notebook and do some daydreaming. Over the years, I've ticked off a multitude of things from my account. The power of this simple technique never ceases to amaze me.

Situations won't always unfold as you expect and sometimes events will surpass your expectations. Bigger goals may take time to achieve, so be patient and don't take your eye off your vision.

5. Spend More Time 'Being'

> *"It is not just do do do. It is not just be be be. It is do be do be do be"*
> - Dr Amit Goswami

If you watch chimps and gorillas, our closest relatives in the animal kingdom, with whom we share around 98% of our DNA, you'll see that they spend lots of time lounging around and relaxing. I believe our need for rest and relaxation is no different.

Physicist Amit Goswami recommends spending much more time simply 'being' - in other words, doing nothing. He says we should alternate our 'doing' with periods of 'being' - what he calls 'do-be-do-be-do-be'. Time spent 'being', he says, is essential for creativity and living a happy life.

Our culture places huge emphasis on 'doing' - the old stress-struggle approach we talked of before. I come from a family of workaholics and the need to be constantly 'doing' was so deeply ingrained that it's taken years for me to stop feeling guilty when I take time to relax.

> *"It's the moments that I have stopped just to be, rather than do, that have given me true happiness. Try it. Be still. Be present. There's a reason we're called human beings and not human doings."*
> - Richard Branson

Constant 'doing' is often very counterproductive. The human brain needs periods of down-time. These periods often bring useful intuitions which we miss if we don't stop to relax. When we relax, we tune to a frequency that's more resonant with the experience of love and abundance and we're more likely to receive guidance. You may have a 'Eureka' moment where a solution, or urge to take action, suddenly comes to mind. There are many stories of scientific breakthroughs being made during moments of quiet relaxation.

If you find yourself at a crossroads where you can't decide what to do next, spend some time relaxing. I guarantee a path will appear. You may, for example, have an intuition about your relationship situation. You, and only you, have the answers to *all* your dilemmas - there's really no need to consult anyone else because the answers will come from within if you quieten your mind.

The more you relax and let go, the more you radiate the feeling that you *already* have what you want. This really is the secret to success and creating an abundant life. This is when the things you've been so desperately wanting often start to show up.

If you had everything you wanted, you'd be spending a lot more time relaxing and 'being' because there'd be no need to chase desperately after your dreams. If you're constantly 'doing', you're actually broadcasting that you *do not* currently have what you're trying so hard to achieve.

Many people spend little, or no, time in the 'being' state. If you're so busy that you can't relax and do nothing for a few moments each day, then your life is extremely out of balance. Meditation is the ultimate form of being. However, simply sitting, or lying down, without engaging in activities or thought can be just as blissful - no phone or TV allowed!

6. Other Ways to Lift Your Mood

Here are some other ways to lift your mood - some of these will come naturally as you feel better:

- Laughter

> *"We have an infinite number of reasons to be happy*
> *and a serious responsibility not to be serious."*
> - Maharishi Yogi

Life doesn't have to be serious. Laughter really is the best medicine. This is a muscle we need to exercise regularly. As comedian Ken Dodd has wisely pointed out:

> *"We're all born with a chuckle muscle, and if you exercise it every day it'll keep you young and frisky all your life, but if you don't it dries up and drops off!"*

Make it your intention to laugh more, and laughter will find you. Remember to hold on to, and amplify, those happy feelings to ensure more laughter comes your way.

- Uplifting Music

Music is a great tool for arousing emotion, as long as it's music that's uplifting or relaxing, rather than sad and melancholy. I regularly use music to tune to a joyful or uplifting frequency.

- Your Physical Health

It's impossible to resonate with happy circumstances if you're chronically stressed, exhausted and run down - like simply attracts like. Good sleep, physical exercise and healthy eating will greatly improve your wellbeing.

As you tune to a more positive frequency, your health is likely to improve anyway. You won't be resonant with junk food and disturbed sleep if you're feeling happy. When I cleaned up my inner state, my asthma dramatically improved and my sugar and coffee addictions fell away, with little effort. During my depression years, I struggled desperately to overcome these issues, without success. My inner state had to change *first*, before these problems could resolve.

Physical exercise is also a great way to change your energy. All sorts of positive outer manifestations took place when I improved my fitness levels. Just a few tiny lifestyle changes can pave the way for bigger changes.

- Take up a New Hobby

Distracting yourself with a new interest or hobby is a wonderful way to 'Let Go and Let God'. It diverts your attention *away* from your relationship anxieties, allowing your situation to change or resolve.

- Spend Time in Nature

Nature has a healing frequency compared to an over-crowded and polluted city. Being in nature helps you take on this frequency. Even the biggest cities have green spaces where you can sit and focus on the subtle sounds and smells of nature - the rustling of leaves and trees, birds singing, insects buzzing and the scent of flowers.

There's a harmony and intelligence to nature - plants, insects and animals go about their business effortlessly and peacefully. This is how we're meant to live too. We're part of nature and not separate from it.

- Take A Holiday

Taking a holiday distracts you from your problems and helps you forget your relationship situation back home. You may find that when you return from holiday, circumstances have magically shifted or resolved.

- Tackle Your Procrastinations

Do you have lots of annoying tasks that you put off doing - sometimes for years? Procrastination causes a chronic background stress that lowers our mood, particularly if we keep observing each day the things we're putting off.

Writing a list of everything you're avoiding and ruthlessly working your way through it, can be hugely uplifting. I did this recently and the relief was enormous. Five minutes spent on a project per day, equates to about thirty hours a year, so you can achieve a lot with a small daily investment. This approach has allowed me to transform my garden and finish a painting I started ten years ago.

- **Declutter**

When I first started cleaning up my thinking, I was seized with powerful urges to clean my home and throw out all my clutter. My inner world was changing dramatically and my outer world, it seemed, wanted to reflect this.

I attacked cupboards, drawers, shelves, filing cabinets and wardrobes and deleted old emails and files from my computer. Never before, or since, have I had such a radical purge and it was hugely cathartic.

Your home environment usually reflects your inner world. You can often gauge someone's emotional state by visiting their home. A depressed state can lead to chaos and clutter. As you clean up your inner world, don't be surprised if you get urges to clean up your outer world. Change *your* frequency and your outer world will seek to come into resonance with that new frequency.

8: Learning to Radiate Love

"If you want to be loved, the way to get it is to love. It is not only the very best method but it is the only method. To receive love we must love because what we give out must come back."

- Lester Levenson

O nce you've cultivated a happier and more peaceful inner state, you can start to reach for the loving feelings at the upper end of the scale. It's these feelings which *really* magnetize you for love.

As long as you desperately *need* to be loved, you will never be a match to a healthy loving relationship. Change your focus from *getting* love to *giving* love, and you'll start to attract love from all around you.

Learning to love, without needing to receive it, is the route to health and happiness. When we're desperate to be loved, we suffer and we repel the love we're so desperately seeking. However, when we're the one who is loving, we feel happy and we attract love back. Learning to be more loving is a skill we can all develop. When you radiate love, you can't help but attract love. Love attracts love.

What Is Love?

First, let's clear up some common misunderstandings about love:

- **Conditional Versus Unconditional Love**

  It took me years to discover that there's a much healthier love than the very toxic variety I used to be so familiar with. Healthy relationships are based on what we call 'unconditional love'. Here, your love flows outwards from wholeness and happiness - you feel good about yourself, you generate your own happiness, and you let your partner be themselves without conditions attached. This is the kind of love I experience now, but things used to be very different.

  My old relationships were based on 'conditional' or 'co-dependent' love. I was needy and depressed and thought it was my partner's job to make me happy. I didn't feel worthy of love and constantly feared rejection. I needed my partner to treat me in a certain way, otherwise I suffered. My focus was always on *getting* rather than *giving* love.

  It's important to understand this difference between conditional and unconditional love. It's the unconditional variety we need to cultivate. When you feel how good it feels to love unconditionally, you won't want to love any other way.

- **Lust Is Not Love**

  It's easy to confuse sexual feelings with love and this is a common mistake. Sex can certainly open the door to love, but sexual feelings are not the same as loving feelings. Sex together with love is a beautiful combination. However, you can feel love without sex, and you can have sex without love

  Sex can, of course, be very pleasurable. However, we know from Chapter 5 that pleasure is temporary and doesn't bring lasting happiness. Remove sex from the equation, and love is a feeling you can experience in *any* relationship, not just with your partner.

- ### There's No Shortage of Love

It's important to realise that there's no shortage of love. Our culture promotes the faulty belief that finding a soulmate is our only route to true love and happiness. When we see our partner as our *only* source of love, it puts an enormous burden on them and closes us off to love in our platonic relationships. It also makes us see love as hard to find and in short supply.

It's these faulty beliefs about love which make us so devastated when a relationship ends - we feel we've lost love forever. In fact, nothing could be further from the truth. You can't lose love. Your capacity to love and be loved remains intact. Love is everywhere. It's within you and everyone around you - waiting to be expressed.

You never need to chase after love - chasing it is the very best way to repel it. Become resonant with love *first* and love will find you. When you're in a loving state, you'll see love everywhere and attract it back in equal measure - people, and even animals, will be drawn to you.

- ### How to Become Resonant with a Loving Relationship

Love is really just a heightened state of happiness. Creating a still and peaceful mind is the foundation for happiness, and we've discussed ways of doing this already. Cultivating an outward flow of love can then be practiced once your inner state has quietened.

Loving feelings come in many subtle shades - practice any of these and you'll become resonant with loving experiences such as the rekindling of a relationship. Be warned - you may attract new potential partners the more you practice this! Here are some ways to become resonant with a loving relationship:

1. Make Your Friendships More Loving

> *"Friendship is the purest love. It is the highest form of Love where nothing is asked for, no condition, where one simply enjoys giving."*
> - Osho

Loving feelings are usually most intense in a romantic relationship.

However, you can also feel love towards friends, relatives, work colleagues, neighbours, pets, and even complete strangers. The more you practice this outward flow of platonic love, the more loving you'll become and the more love you'll receive back.

You may discover that platonic love is just as fulfilling as romantic love, if not more so. Although less intense, there's usually a lot less heartache involved.

It's easy when we're engrossed in an intense love relationship to let friendships fall away. I was guilty of this in the past. I was so desperate for love that I wanted to spend every moment with my partner, to the exclusion of everyone else. This placed great pressure on my partner and created an unhealthy dependence. I stopped investing in friendships and some of these, regrettably, fell away.

Filling up on platonic love reduces neediness. This is why platonic relationships are so important. If you're in a relationship, your partner will pick up on this lack of neediness and is likely to respond more lovingly towards you.

2. Make Your Romantic Relationship More Platonic

Often, we're more tolerant of our friends' behaviour than our partner's. If you see your partner as a friend - first and foremost - you put your relationship with them on an equal footing with your friendships and relax all those heavy expectations which can be so stifling in a romantic relationship.

Great suffering comes from putting your partner on a pedestal. It can then be devastating if they slip up, or fall short, in some way. See them as a friend, rather than your reason for living, and you'll have a much healthier kind of love.

The secret is, therefore, to make your platonic relationships more loving, and your romantic relationship more platonic.

3. Practice an Outward Flow of Love

Here are some ways to cultivate an outward flow of love:

a) With Strangers

A great place to practice is with complete strangers. As you walk down the street, or when you buy groceries, see if you can feel some warmth towards people you don't know.

We have an immense amount in common with *every* other human on the planet. We're all entangled on a quantum level and we're all going through this miraculous thing called 'life'. Without exception, we all want to be happy.

Try to spot things to appreciate in those you encounter each day - nice eyes, a friendly face or a pleasing smile - everyone has something to appreciate. This trains you to be less critical of others and to see the good rather than the bad.

People will tune into your more loving demeanour and want to interact with you. You'll attract smiles, offers of help and other friendly gestures. This is the world I experience now. This friendly feedback is a sign that you're tuning to a more loving frequency.

If you want to supercharge this, try saying silently in your head - *"I love you"* - to anyone you encounter during your day. This may feel ridiculous at first, but it becomes enjoyable when you notice the friendly response it seems to elicit.

b) With Those You Already Know

Then there are those who are already in your life - friends, family, and work colleagues (again, we'll leave out your partner in case this stirs up painful feelings). Spend some time thinking about these people and what you appreciate about them. Some will be easier to love than others but see if you can still conjure some loving feelings. Perhaps imagine giving them a hug, sharing a joke or telling them you love them.

This is also a great way to heal difficult relationships - sometimes miraculously, and often without any direct contact with the other person. There's no better way to repair a difficult relationship than to cultivate love towards that person.

c) On the Road

We've all heard of 'road rage' and you may have felt rage towards other drivers yourself. I used to be a very impatient driver. Being enclosed in a powerful machine seems to make us less courteous than we usually are. Road rage is unpleasant and unnecessary and brings no joy to anyone.

So, a wonderful place to practice loving kindness is on the road. I get great pleasure now from giving way to other cars, and thanking those who do the same for me.

d) With Animals and Children

Animals, such as cats and dogs, can be very affectionate and appreciative of loving gestures - so, too, can young children. They offer us true unconditional love and we can learn a lot from them about how to be more loving.

e) Through Giving

Giving of any kind is an act of love. Learning to give more freely, without the need for anything in return, is a big part of becoming more loving. If you feel motivated to do so - offer help, offer your time, be courteous, be charitable and give thanks, praise, gifts, compliments and compassion.

f) Through Loving Meditation

Loving-kindness meditation - or 'Metta Bhavana' - is a central practice of Buddhism. This involves cultivating loving feelings towards others by quietening your mind and feeling love radiating from your heart. You don't have to meditate to do this - you can practice it as you go about your day.

4. Love Yourself

"One has just to be oneself. The moment you accept yourself as you are, all burdens, all mountainous burdens, simply disappear. Then life is a sheer joy, a festival of lights"
- Shree Rajneesh

The most important relationship, above all others, is the one you have with yourself. Learning to love yourself restores harmony to *all* your relationships.

If you don't love and accept yourself, you'll find that situations arise to confirm this - rejection from a partner is a good example. A feeling of unworthiness becomes a self-fulfilling prophecy and others will tend to react to you accordingly.

I used to think that if I could just find someone who truly loved me, *then* I'd feel good about myself. This, of course, is back-to-front logic. The self-love must come from within *before* we can expect to see it reflected back from others.

The truth is, we're all uniquely perfect just as we are. Nothing needs to be changed or improved. Real joy comes from simply being ourselves in our truest sense, as nature made us. There's no need to try to be something we're not. When we're completely at ease in our own skin we are at our most attractive.

A lack of self-worth is what fuels a desperate need to be loved. If we didn't feel loved as a child, we tend to carry this unloved feeling into adulthood. Fortunately, it's never too late to start loving yourself. Here are some ways to nurture this feeling:

a) Watch Out for Moments When you Feel Insecure

Watch closely for moments when you *don't* feel good about yourself. This requires great self-awareness - these old feelings usually slip by without you noticing.

Often specific situations trigger our feelings of low self-worth. A few days ago, I caught my reflection in a shop window, and this set off a cascade of old feelings of unworthiness. Fortunately, I instantly spotted these feelings and was able to remind myself that this was old programming which I could let go of.

The more you catch these moments, the less they'll happen, and the better you'll start to feel about yourself. Remind yourself in these moments that you're enough, just as you are. No one else expects perfection in you, and I'm sure you don't expect perfection in others.

I've also found this method very useful for tackling my social anxiety. I watch closely for the old faulty thinking that comes up in social situations. Like most of my 'problems', at the root of my social anxiety was some very faulty thinking which brought years of misery.

It's also worked wonders for me romantically. I now have a partner who accepts me as I am, and who I can be myself with. Again, repetition is essential. Keep chipping away at this and you'll soon see the real 'you' emerging.

b) Attractiveness Isn't About Your Looks

"If you have good thoughts they will shine out of your face like sunbeams and you will always look lovely"
- Roald Dahl

Our culture places huge emphasis on physical appearance. Good looks are promoted as essential for love, happiness and success. Cosmetic surgery is more popular than ever, and we see celebrities using it to change or hold onto their looks. However, this is seeking self-worth in the *wrong* place. Unless you're disfigured in some way, cosmetic surgery won't have much impact on how you feel about yourself. You may get a temporary boost but not lasting self-esteem.

The perfect body won't bring romantic success. We see this in the turbulent love lives of many 'good looking' celebrities. Good looks won't make you loveable - you have to feel loveable on the inside first. Self-worth is an inner state which we must nurture.

What's interesting is that when you *do* start feeling better about yourself, your outer appearance may well change to reflect this. You may become more energetic, have a healthier glow, lose weight, eat more healthily, take exercise or wear new clothes. Feeling good about yourself on the inside really does seem to alter the way you look on the outside. However, the inner state - *as always* - must come first.

c) Carry A Mental Image of Yourself That You Like

While looks are unimportant, what you *think* you look like *is* important. We tend to carry a visual image of ourselves in our mind. If this isn't a favourable one, it'll affect your confidence and how others treat you. Even those blessed with good looks can feel ugly, or insecure about their appearance.

Part of loving yourself on the inside, involves making peace with what you see on the outside. It's important to accept and appreciate your body.

When you look in the mirror, try to look less critically and more lovingly at yourself. Only a tiny minority conform to the stereotypical 'perfect' body that's portrayed in the media. Instead of focusing on what you *don't* like about your body, focus on what you *do* like.

I used to have a constant inner battle with my appearance, bordering on the obsessional. My self-esteem hinged entirely on what I saw in the mirror each day and how much I weighed. If I didn't like what I saw, I'd carry this negative mental image for the rest of the day and it hugely affected my confidence. Compliments from others never seemed to change the way I felt about myself.

It took me a long time to shake off this unhelpful programming and to realise that the real 'me' was quite separate from, and independent of, my body. I still make an effort with my appearance, but my self-esteem no longer hinges on it. I've learnt to focus on feeling good about myself on the inside first, rather than trying to change my appearance *in order to* feel good about myself.

A useful exercise is to find a photograph of yourself that you like.

Look lovingly at this person and try to carry this image in your mind, *rather* than the less favourable one you may see in the mirror in the morning. Remind yourself of your photograph, whenever you catch yourself feeling unattractive. By repeatedly substituting your negative mental image with a more favourable one, you'll start to radiate a more loving energy, and you may well attract compliments.

Can you visualize the 'best' version of yourself? How does it feel to be this person? Practice this feeling and you'll start to morph into this person. Soon, you'll start to see this better version of yourself reflected in the mirror and in the responses of those around you.

d) Be Your Own Cheerleader

It feels good to receive praise from others, but you really don't need anyone else to boost your self-esteem. If you desperately crave reassurance from others, as I used to, you're unlikely to receive it.

Instead, regularly pat yourself on the back and be your own cheerleader. Then you won't need reassurance from others. Ironically, that's when you're most likely to receive the positive feedback that you used to crave.

5. Cultivate Loving Feelings With Your Imagination

Loving feelings come in many different shades - you can feel loving, loved, lovable, 'in love' - with lots of subtle variations in between. Repeatedly conjuring these feelings with your imagination is what really magnetizes you for love.

Do this consistently, and you'll start to notice others responding more lovingly towards you. You don't need to be in a permanent state of lovingness to experience more love in your life. However, the more you practice, the more love you'll attract.

Wallowing in loving feelings is what we do naturally when we're 'in love' - we fantasise about future moments with our partner. In other words, your partner's presence is not necessary for you to tap into these feelings - your imagination can do it all by itself.

You can visualise anyone for this exercise - real or imagined - but, once again, avoid your partner if this stirs up painful feelings. The best time to practice is when you're *already* feeling good. Don't attempt this if your mood is low.

Let's look at feeling 'loved'. Shut your eyes and imagine something that makes you feel loved - perhaps the sensation of someone's arm around you, leaning your head on someone's shoulder, a kiss on the cheek or being given a hug. Keep rehearsing these feelings regularly and you'll change your default frequency to a more loving one.

With practice, you'll get better at holding these loving feelings for longer. Over time, you can build a library of mental images and memories to help with this. Immerse yourself regularly in these feelings and outer experiences will soon reflect it back.

Don't forget to monitor yourself for any angry, judgmental or critical thoughts or feelings. These are not compatible with a loving frequency.

As I mentioned previously, before I met my current partner, John, I was single for about four years. During this period, I worked diligently on my thinking and on cultivating loving feelings. From a place of intense suffering, I slowly transformed my inner state to one of deep peace and contentedness.

From this more loving state, it became easier to wallow in loving feelings, even though I wasn't in a relationship - I simply fell 'in love' with life. It was during this time that John showed up. I'm certain that my new more loving vibration, along with the step we'll look at next, is what made me resonant with this much healthier and happier relationship.

6. Live As If You're *Already* In A Loving Relationship

"Men do not attract that which they
want, but that which they are."
- James Allen

I recently heard about a woman who met and married her soulmate after living 'as if' her ideal partner was *already* in her life. She really got into the minute details of what this would entail. She looked for birthday cards and presents to buy him, she set a place for him at the dinner table each night, she bought new outfits, planned where they'd go on dates, and arranged her home so there was space for him. She even started choosing her engagement ring and planning her wedding. She really became resonant with the feeling of being in a loving relationship and, sure enough, like attracted like and her soulmate showed up.

Living 'as if', means you mentally step into the reality of the life you want to lead. Instead of imagining this as something that *might* happen in the future, you become that person now. Do this consistently, and for long enough, and your subconscious starts to believe that this is your current reality. The outer circumstances then follow.

It's this principle that James Allen's quote is referring to. You won't attract love by desperately *wanting* it - you must become the person who *already* feels loving and loved. Stop wanting and, instead, start dreaming, acting, pretending, imagining and fantasising. Children are naturally good at this - it's time to start daydreaming again.

Try to imagine how you'd feel if you were *already* in a loving relationship. Again, try to avoid thinking about your partner for this exercise. Is there anything you've stopped doing because you're no longer in a relationship? If your ideal partner arrived on your doorstep now - are you ready for them? If not, what steps do you need to take?

Have you stopped wearing your best clothes? Are you changing your bedding or cleaning your home less often? Perhaps you've stopped going to the gym, flossing your teeth, having your hair cut or planning activities you enjoy? Do you walk and talk differently when you're in a happy relationship?

This isn't just about imagining, it's about *actually* doing those things you'd be doing if you were already in a relationship. This may sound like madness, but it really does work, not just with love but with any new situation you'd like to experience. I've heard of many success stories with this technique and have used it successfully myself.

Before I met John, I'd really begun to believe that a loving relationship was a possibility and I started preparing for him in my life. Sure enough, John showed up. I had an impulse, one day, to attend a local meditation class for the first time - we both acted on the same impulse that day and the rest unfolded naturally - no trying or searching was needed.

9: Keeping the Honeymoon Phase Alive

"I learned again and again in my life, until you get your own act together, you're not ready for Big Love. What you're ready for is one of those co-dependent relationships where you desperately need a partner."

- Dr Bruce Lipton

Rekindling your relationship is one thing - maintaining the relationship is another. If your relationship *does* reignite, or you find a new partner, there are some very useful techniques for sustaining love which we'll look at in this chapter.

Being happy is the *most* essential ingredient for maintaining a happy relationship and we've already talked about how to be happy. However, there are some other important skills you can learn.

Get Your Partner On Board If You Can

If you can get your partner on board with this chapter, so much the better. If you can't - don't worry. As you change yourself and the way you relate to your partner - they, too, will change.

Maintaining the Honeymoon Phase

During the blissful honeymoon phase, we feel 'in love', we have boundless energy and we radiate health and happiness. Unfortunately, this phase is often short-lived, and can even turn from love into hate.

How can we stop this happening? Biologist Dr Bruce Lipton, in his book *The Honeymoon Effect*, shows us how we can recapture the honeymoon period so that a happily-ever-after scenario becomes possible. This is all about becoming conscious of those deeply programmed unconscious thoughts and feelings which get us into trouble.

As already mentioned, I've been in a happy long-term relationship for the last ten years and we have a very blissful connection of a kind I've not experienced before. This has come about through religiously practicing everything we've talked about so far, along with the techniques in this chapter.

Why Does the Honeymoon Phase Wear Off?

One of the major reasons why the honeymoon period wears off, as Bruce Lipton highlights in his book, is that we stop monitoring our behaviour. In the honeymoon phase, we make a conscious effort to impress our partner, to look good, and to be attentive and loving - and our partner does the same. In other words, both partners are on their *very best* behaviour.

It's this careful self-monitoring which stops those ugly and impulsive knee-jerk reactions we're all guilty of when our guard slips. Being mindful of our behaviour allows us to be the most loving version of ourselves.

Focusing on each other's positive qualities is another important ingredient of the honeymoon phase. We also tend to be much happier during this phase, free from anxieties about the future and more present in the moment. It's under these conditions that love really blossoms.

The First Argument

The honeymoon feelings usually continue until this self-monitoring slips for a moment and an ugly behaviour or habit rears its head. This may trigger the first argument. Had this behaviour emerged on the first date, the chance of a second date would have ended in an instant.

The first argument can be a horrifying moment for couples in the honeymoon phase. The love bubble bursts with a loud pop. In my case, it was always the start of a rollercoaster of ecstatic ups and painful downs, until the relationship ended.

I remember the first argument in one of my most toxic relationships during my twenties. I was about to have a romantic dinner with my boyfriend at his flat - let's call him Peter. As I helped Peter set the table, I brushed a crumb from the table onto the floor. Peter spotted me doing this and exclaimed in horror: *"I can't believe you just did that"*. Bemused, I replied: *"I can't believe you just said that"*. The atmosphere deteriorated rapidly, and I left hastily, without dinner, feeling utterly heartbroken.

It seemed Peter was rather obsessive when it came to cleanliness and, until this incident, he'd managed to conceal this from me. It turned out that his mother was the same and he'd learned this behaviour early on. My mother, on the other hand, was always very relaxed in this area.

Despite our unpromising start, Peter and I stayed together, turbulently, for five years. However, our trivial domestic differences caused a permanent tension during our time together. He saw me as slovenly and undomesticated, while I saw him as obsessive and unreasonable.

If only we'd realised we were each behaving according to our different childhood programming, we could have laughed off these incidents, instead of taking it all so personally and enduring years of conflict.

However, cleanliness wasn't the only source of conflict with Peter. I'd had a previous boyfriend who'd been unfaithful, and this led to some irrational knee-jerk behaviours from me when I started seeing Peter. If I saw him glance at an attractive woman, or if he went out socially without me, I'd suffer terribly. This caused great disharmony between us and caused problems in my subsequent relationships. I tried to suppress these strong visceral emotions, but they tended to leak out later, or trigger arguments about something else.

Your Reptile Brain

Our knee-jerk behaviours are usually triggered by primitive 'reptilian' parts of the brain which evolved long ago to help us survive. When the reptile brain sees a threat, it triggers the fight or flight response so that we take appropriate action. While some reptile responses can be useful, many of them cause havoc in non-threatening situations.

For example, we see the reptile brain in action during road rage incidents. A car cuts in front of us and the reptile brain sees this as a threat to its survival, triggering an aggressive response. The conscious brain, which could have rationalised the situation, doesn't get a look-in once the reptile brain takes over.

And it's the reptile brain which can cause trouble for us romantically. Specific situations can spark a jealous rage or make us argue our corner as if our life depended on it. It's the reptile brain which tempts people into having affairs when the rational brain knows this could end a marriage, or break up a family. Again, the reptile brain is at work when we mindlessly reach for unhealthy foods when consciously we're trying not to. It's as though we literally have two minds.

During the honeymoon phase, when we're on our best behaviour, we consciously interrupt our unhelpful knee-jerk reptile responses and it's this that allows love to blossom.

Interrupting Your Knee-Jerk Responses

> *"Until you make the unconscious conscious, it will*
> *direct your life and you will call it fate"*
> - Carl Jung

When the self-monitoring of the honeymoon phase starts to slip, couples often fall into a pattern of arguing and criticizing. I'm sure many relationships could be saved if couples knew the importance of doing what comes naturally during the honeymoon phase - that is, to be extremely mindful of their behaviour when they're together.

Simply observing yourself closely, allows you to interrupt your unhelpful responses. With practice, this becomes a habit. You can also observe your partner's knee-jerk responses - perhaps to something you say or do. Remind yourself that it's their reptile brain you're dealing with in these situations.

At first, you may still react negatively to things your partner says or does. If you do, simply watch yourself reacting and observe your thoughts and feelings. Also, watch for stories that your mind creates about the situation. You don't need to buy into these - they're just stories. Each time you interrupt yourself, your emotional reaction to that particular trigger will reduce.

This takes self-discipline. However, eliminating these knee-jerk behaviours can transform even the most toxic relationship. Congratulate yourself each time you successfully short-circuit a reptile impulse.

Now, here's the good news. When you *do* make peace with a specific situation that used to make you angry or upset, that situation is likely to resolve or disappear. That's because you've stopped stoking it with energy and you're no longer broadcasting those specific emotionally charged 'qwiffs'. This means you're no longer resonant with that experience.

For example, if you make peace with your partner's annoying habit of leaving dishes festering in the sink, you're no longer resonant with the experience of your partner leaving dishes festering in the sink. Your partner is likely to stop leaving dishes in the sink, or they may do so less often. Remarkably, you may find that your partner changes their behaviour without you ever having to confront them.

Becoming conscious of all your 'hot' issues is a powerful way to restore harmony in your relationship and, indeed, to *all* areas of your life.

Get To Know Your Reptile Brain

With practice, you'll get to know your reptile brain and how it ticks - it's often the same triggers that cause it to over-react. Try to mentally separate yourself from it and watch it from a distance. It's not who you *really* are. You may even find humour in this if you can get your partner on board. I can sometimes be heard saying: *"Sorry, that wasn't me - it was my reptile brain"*.

As you keep interrupting your old habitual reactions, the neural pathways enabling those behaviours will start to wither away. More helpful pathways will then develop in their place.

I no longer feel anger while driving. I've also short-circuited my primitive urges to overeat by closely observing and sitting with these urges repeatedly and realising that I don't have to act on them. As a result, I've lost the extra weight I never managed to shed with conventional dieting.

Agree Rather Than Defend

> *"When you have no point to defend, you do not allow the birth of an argument."*
> - Deepak Chopra

Another wonderful technique to master is the art of agreeing, rather than defending. The stubborn reptile brain will defend its corner at the slightest threat - this is how arguments begin. Agreeing, rather than defending, is a powerful way to side-step an argument. Again, this takes self-discipline but it's exhilarating when you pull it off.

Often, we get defensive when we know there's a grain of truth to the comment or accusation that makes us overreact. When Peter reprimanded me for sweeping a crumb on the floor, I flew into defence-mode and tried to fight my corner as if my survival was under threat. Why did I react so strongly when most people would have shrugged the incident off?

The truth is, Peter's comments touched a nerve. Deep down, I knew I was a little undomesticated. I was already dreaming of marriage and babies with Peter and I felt he was questioning my home-making abilities. To my reptile brain this was a serious threat - Peter might reject me, and my dreams of motherhood might never materialise. Of course, I didn't need to interpret the crumb situation in such devastating terms. I'm sure a very different scenario would have unfolded if I'd simply agreed by saying:

> *"Yes, you're right - I am a bit slovenly but I'm going to work on it!"*

When you agree, you disarm your attacker and change the tone of the interaction. What often happens is that your partner then comes to your defence. Not only do you come out feeling good, but you also get your partner on your side. If you have difficulty agreeing with your partner, see if there's a tiny grain of truth in their comment or accusation.

Unfortunately, I didn't master this skill while I was with Peter. Whenever he commented on my domestic failings, my knee-jerk defensiveness and endless brooding on the subject, ensured I was an exact match to more of the same. Predictably, these disagreements continued until the day we parted.

Remember: you get *more* of what you focus your energy and attention upon. Had I not been bothered in the slightest about the crumb incident, this area of conflict wouldn't have repeated. If you're emotionally neutral about a situation, it unlikely to keep recurring.

Listening to your partner in a non-defensive way nurtures those wonderful honeymoon feelings. With practice, your new 'agreeing' response will become hardwired, replacing the old defence response.

Reinterpreting an Area of Conflict

We discussed the power of reinterpreting in Chapter 6. This can also prevent repeating arguments. Tell a *better* story about an area of conflict, and the situation is likely to resolve or disappear. Once reinterpreted, mentally drop the issue like a hot coal. If the conflict returns, remind yourself of your new interpretation and continue to drop the issue mentally. I could have avoided years of conflict with Peter had I looked at our domestic differences more rationally, and not taken the situation so personally.

Change the Way You Look at Your Partner

When you change the way you see your partner, they will change the way they respond to you. Here are some ways to do this:

a) Observe Your Partner's Positive Qualities

Dwelling on our partner's good qualities is what we do naturally during the honeymoon phase and it's a vital part of falling in love. However, we must *continue* to do this to maintain those early loving feelings. All too often, our attention drifts to our partner's annoying habits. This often ends the honeymoon period, or the relationship itself.

I know of no more powerful way of repairing a troubled relationship than to write down a list of your partner's good points. You may feel a surge of love for them after doing this, and your partner will sense this. If you can get your partner to do this exercise too, you'll *really* recapture those loving feelings. If only my parents could have practised this!

Here are some questions to ask yourself as you do this exercise:

- *What do you love about your partner?*
- *What are they doing right?*
- *What are they good at?*
- *Is there anything about them you take for granted?*

It's also important to quickly shift your attention *away* from any perceived negatives. Don't dwell on the one thing they're doing wrong, when they're doing many other things right.

I wish I'd known about this technique when I was with Peter. Near the end of our relationship, I started logging in a notebook all the things he was doing to upset me - his critical comments about my domestic failings, his lack of attentiveness and unwillingness to help me. I'd then confront him with these complaints and plead with him to stop.

It's no surprise that this approach only seemed to bring *more* of the same. Of course, this was because I was focusing intensely on what I *didn't* want. Predictably, the relationship fell apart soon after my notebook logging phase and he left me for someone else.

There are probably many things about your partner that you've completely overlooked. When I tried to think of some extra positives about my current partner, John, I was amazed at how many I came up with. Improve the thoughts and feelings you're broadcasting in relation to your partner and you become resonant with a much happier relationship.

b) Relate to Your Partner As a Friend

We've already discussed in Chapter 8 the importance of relating to your partner as a friend, first and foremost. This makes you relax your conditions and expectations. Taking this pressure off your partner makes you more tolerant of their behaviour and fosters a healthier unconditional kind of love.

c) Men Are From Mars, Women Are From Venus

"When men and women are able to respect and accept their differences then love has a chance to blossom"
- John Gray

John Gray's famous book *Men Are From Mars, Women Are From Venus*, shows us that conflict often arises because men and women are simply different. Being aware of these differences can *greatly* improve your relationship.

Often, we take it personally if our partner behaves in a certain way. However, this behaviour may be one that's common to men or women around the world - one that evolved millions of years ago because it conferred a survival advantage during our cave-dwelling days.

Back then, men went off to hunt while women stayed at home to deal with child rearing and domestic chores. Men who were aggressive, self-centred and driven to succeed were more likely to survive, so those traits were passed on, while men who were sensitive and empathic were more likely to be killed off. However, nurturing and empathic traits were useful in women because they helped in the rearing of offspring.

Whether we like it or not, our behaviour is still very much governed by these ancient genetically programmed traits - a few decades of feminism isn't going to undo millions of years of evolution.

Of course, we don't all conform to these gender differences. They're just *tendencies*, but it's well worth being aware of them. Let's look at some of the most obvious ones.

If you're a man:

- *Don't judge a woman if she's needy or wants constant reassurance. Women need to be sure that you'll stick around to protect and provide if you have children - that's why this tendency evolved.*

- *If she's unhappy or upset, don't get angry, defensive, feel blamed or distance yourself - this will make her more upset.*

- *Women like to talk about their problems and be listened to with empathy. A woman enjoys talking for its own sake. She does this to get close to you, not because she wants you to give solutions.*

- *Don't feel neglected if she's taken up with child-rearing - the instinct to nurture can be all-consuming for women and has evolved because it ensured the survival of offspring.*

If you're a woman:

- *Don't judge a man if he seems insensitive, uncommunicative, self-centred, unapologetic or disinterested. These traits helped men to survive long ago. His instinct is to look after himself, even if it means sacrificing others.*

- *Don't judge a man if he offers solutions rather than listens to your problems. Men like to demonstrate their competence.*

- *Don't offer unsolicited advice to a man - it can undermine his need to feel competent.*

- *When men do communicate, they like to get to the point and will only want to listen if they feel the conversation has a point.*

- *Men need to feel needed and may feel neglected if you seem overly absorbed in child-rearing.*

- *Don't think he doesn't care if he appears more focused on his work or hobbies than on you. Success, achievement and power are very important to a man.*

- *Don't feel rejected if your partner withdraws physically or emotionally for short periods into his 'cave'. Men often do this when they're stressed. Allow him to withdraw, without chasing after him. When he returns, he may be more willing to listen and offer love, and this is often the best time to start a conversation.*

Being aware of these differences stops us judging our partner harshly for their apparently alien behaviour and allows us to meet each other somewhere in the middle. Women can't expect men to behave as women do, and vice versa.

Change the Way You See Your 'Relationship'

Not only can you change the way you see your partner, but you can also change the way you see your 'relationship', as follows:

a) **See Your Relationship as a Form of Personal Development**

> *"Whenever your relationship is not working, whenever it brings out the 'madness' in you and in your partner, be glad."*
> - Eckhart Tolle

Relationships often bring issues to the surface that are already there. That's why being in a relationship can seem to magnify our pain. This causes some people to avoid relationships altogether, while it prompts others to endlessly change partners in the hope it'll be better with someone else.

The reality is, no one else has the power to make you suffer. It's not your partner who causes you pain - it's *you* and your thoughts, feelings, perceptions and expectations.

Your relationship is a wonderful opportunity for self-improvement. Conflict is a wake-up call. It alerts you to faulty thoughts and stories lurking unconsciously that need uprooting.

As I mentioned earlier, I broke-up with my current partner, John, a year into our relationship. This was due to some trust issues I'd developed with previous partners. When I started seeing John, these old insecurities resurfaced. My fear of rejection, and not being worthy, started playing repetitively in my mind. This led to arguments and caused John to walk away from the relationship.

During our six months apart, I mentally let go of our relationship and religiously practiced everything we've covered in this book. John eventually initiated contact, of his own accord, and a beautiful rekindling took place. Once back together, I worked on my trust issues by repeatedly observing, reinterpreting and letting go of my faulty thoughts and stories in this area. Things have gone smoothly ever since.

So, welcome your conflict with open arms, for it's a gift in disguise - a chance to let go of your faulty programming and move your relationship to a new level.

b) There are No 'Relationships' - Only 'Relating'

Although I've used the word 'relationship' throughout this book, there's really no such thing as a 'relationship' or 'marriage'. These aren't things we can see or touch. They don't exist, other than as concepts in our mind.

As Eckhart Tolle points out - all we *ever* have is 'relating' in the present moment. Your 'relationship' is simply a series of interactions between you and your partner. This 'relating' in the present moment is all there is, and it's all you really need to pay attention to.

When we think of a relationship or marriage as a 'thing', it creates unspoken expectations about how our partner should behave. We pick up these expectations from the culture around us. For example:

- *you must stay with me forever*
- *you must make me happy*
- *you must always love me*
- *you must not be attracted to anyone else*
- *you are mine*
- *you must behave in certain ways otherwise I'll be unhappy, or I may leave you*

When we marry, we take vows to ensure our partner sticks to these rules. We also seek 'commitment' and 'trust'. Again, these are just mental concepts which we can't see or touch. However, these concepts create lots of unspoken rules which lurk in the background and often lead to conflict.

The secret is to be *truly* present in the moment when you're with your partner, and leave the past, future and all your expectations, conditions and grievances at the door. This makes interactions lighter and more playful. Your partner will *want* to spend time with you, and they'll keep coming back for more.

Couples often get so engrossed with domestic issues that they forget to have fun. A happy relationship is full of laughter. If you're not laughing together, it means there's mental baggage intruding on the present moment - let it go!

When you have fun with your partner, you feel secure, loving and loved. These are the feelings we try to enforce when we seek 'commitment', 'trust' and take marriage vows. However, there's really no need for such rules or conditions because the best way to feel secure, loving and loved is simply to enjoy the present moment together.

So, make your 'relating' of the highest quality and drop your mental baggage in each interaction. This is the only *real* relationship 'work' required for a loving and lasting connection with your partner.

10: Bringing It All Together

"Love is our birthright. Do not go seeking
for that which you are."

- Neville Goddard

W e've covered a lot of material, so in this last chapter we'll go over the most important points again. Repetition is the key to success here - keep practicing these methods until they become part of your day-to-day life. First, though, an important point.

Change Requires Commitment

People often read self-help books, feel a bit better, and then return to their unhappy life without practicing what they've learned. I spent years jumping from book to book, but not actually doing the work. I had a good intellectual understanding, but I wasn't living it. This is like watching a fitness DVD and expecting to get fit without doing the exercises.

It was only when I *really* practiced it - consistently over *many* months - that my life began to turn around. Without a significant change in your inner world, you'll keep experiencing the same old problems - year after year.

Dedicate *at least* a couple of months to the methods we've covered, and your new way of 'being' will begin to take root and your old conditioning will start to fall away. If you apply a single-minded determination to this, you *will* see the results - not just romantically but in all areas of your life.

Let's Summarise

Here are the most important points again:

Early Steps

Emotional outbursts during a break up will only serve to push your partner further away. So, too, will attempts to hold onto your partner, or to control or fix the relationship. Letting go and surrendering to your current situation is the most important first step. Ceasing contact with your partner, until you've made significant progress with the inner work, is also important.

You Created Where You're at Now

Quantum physics is now backing up what ancient religions and philosophies have told us all along - that mind *precedes* matter and not the other way around.

Everything is composed of energy, and like frequencies attract like frequencies. Change your own frequency *first* and your outer circumstances will then change to reflect this. If you want more love, wealth, health and happiness, you *must* grasp this fundamental principle.

What you're going through now is the end product of all you've been thinking and feeling for some time. You're not a victim and you're not unlucky in love. If you can truly understand that you, and *only* you, are creating your reality, all anger, blame and resentment will start to dissolve. This paves the way for a much more loving and forgiving frequency.

Being Happy Creates Happy Circumstances

Cultivating a happy and loving inner state makes you resonant with happy and loving experiences. Heartache can't touch you when you're in this state.

Seeking happiness in another person will *not* bring you happiness. You'll never find happiness outside yourself because your capacity for happiness lies within you. In other words, you *already* have what you're seeking - it's always present, simply waiting to be uncovered. Taking on this fundamental principle stops you desperately *wanting* to be with your partner. And when you stop wanting, the things you used to want so desperately start to show up in your life.

The True Nature of Happiness

Here's a reminder of the true nature of happiness:

- *Happiness is your natural state*
- *Happiness is what arises, in the present moment, from a still and peaceful mind that's free from toxic thoughts and feelings*
- *Happiness must come before happy circumstances can show up*
- *You don't need anything 'out there' to be happy*
- *You won't find happiness in any person, place, event, circumstance or material object*
- *You don't need a partner to be happy*
- *It's not your partner's job to make you happy*
- *Your partner does not cause your happiness or unhappiness - you do*
- *Happiness is not the same as pleasure*
- *Pleasure is a fleeting and temporary state associated with activities like eating a delicious meal or watching a good film*
- *Chasing pleasure in the belief it'll make you happy is a recipe for unhappiness*

The True Nature of Love

And here's a reminder of the true nature of love:

- *There is no shortage of love*
- *It's our need to be loved which causes us to suffer*
- *Focus on giving love, rather than getting love, and you'll attract love back*
- *Healthy relationships are based on unconditional love where we allow our partner to be themselves, without conditions or expectations*
- *Your partner is not your only source of love*
- *Friendship is the purest form of love*
- *Lust is not the same as love*

- *Making your platonic relationships more loving, and your romantic relationships more platonic, reduces dependence on your partner*
- *The less you depend on your partner for love, the more love they're likely to feel for you*

Repairing Your Inner World

Moving from heartache to happiness is a gradual process. Intense suffering can be tackled as follows:

- **Feel Your Feelings**

  Allow yourself to really *feel* your feelings, without fueling them with stories, and they'll soon dissolve. Feelings are simply movements of energy so try not to label them as good or bad. Catch a feeling early and you'll stop it escalating.

- **Dismantle Your Mental Stories**

  It's not the breakdown of a relationship which causes pain but the thoughts and stories we have about it. Becoming aware of these repetitive background thoughts about your relationship situation reduces their frequency. The mind needs daily discipline - keep letting go of your negative thoughts, and happiness will soon follow. Always be mindful of the words you speak and avoid negative conversations about your circumstances.

  As you starve your 'problems' of energy and attention, you'll find they start to resolve or dissolve. This may be through inspired action, or the problem may simply drop from your reality.

Nurturing Happiness

You can nurture your happiness as follows:

- *Spend more time in the present moment*
- *Appreciate what you already have*
- *Keep focusing on what you do want, rather than on what you don't want*
- *Spend less time 'doing' and more time 'being'*
- *Turn towards the positives and away from the negatives*
- *Celebrate anything good that happens to you*

Radiating Love

As your mind quietens, it becomes easier to tune to a more loving frequency. Change your focus from *getting* love to *giving* love and you'll become resonant with loving experiences. This can help the rekindling process and also makes you more attractive to potential new partners.

You can cultivate loving feelings as follows:

- **Practice Platonic Love**

  Platonic love can be felt in any relationship - with friends, neighbours, relatives, work colleagues, animals, children and strangers. Every interaction is an opportunity to practice an outward flow of love.

- **Love Yourself**

  Remember that you are perfect and complete as nature made you - there's no need to change or try to be somebody else. Lovability isn't about your looks - it's about what you radiate. The more you love and accept yourself as you are, the more lovable you become.

  Watch for moments when you feel insecure and know that this is old and faulty programming. Discard these old thoughts and stories about yourself and you'll start to radiate a new energy. Remember to be your own cheerleader rather than seek approval from others.

- **Cultivate Loving Feelings With Your Imagination**

  Create a library of mental images to help you conjure feelings of being loved and lovable. Imagine an arm around your shoulder, for example, or a kiss on the cheek, or a loving embrace.

- **Live As If You're *Already* In A Loving Relationship**

  We attract what we are, and not what we want. How do you act, think, and behave when you're in a loving relationship? The more you live the finer details of this, and continue to behave as if you're *already* in a happy relationship, the more you become resonant with that reality.

Keeping the Honeymoon Phase Alive

If you do reconcile with your partner, or begin a new relationship, the following points can help to keep the honeymoon phase alive:

- *Make your inner state your highest priority*
- *Learn to agree, rather than defend*
- *Become aware of your unhelpful knee-jerk reptile responses*
- *Be aware of male-female behavioural differences*
- *Regularly dwell on your partner's positive qualities*
- *Remember that a 'relationship' or 'marriage' is just a mental concept*
- *All that exists is 'relating' in the present moment*
- *Make your relating in the present moment of the highest quality*
- *If you see your partner as a friend, you become more tolerant and forgiving*
- *Continue to invest in your platonic relationships and make them as loving as you can.*

What If Your Partner Doesn't Initiate Contact?

If you've been rejected by your partner and you long to reunite, it's natural to want *them* to be the one who initiates contact. Change your inner state with the methods we've discussed, and you'll optimize the potential for this to happen.

However, if your partner does *not* initiate contact and you have a strong impulse to contact them - what then? Here, you must rely on your intuition. Only *you* know the precise circumstances of your break up, and whether it feels appropriate to make contact.

It's wise to consider the following points before you do make contact:

- *Only initiate contact if you've felt a significant positive shift in your inner state. This may take a few months, so be sure you've invested enough time in this.*
- *Never contact your partner impulsively - wait a few days to see if the impulse persists.*
- *Taking action out of neediness, fear or desperation is likely to backfire.*
- *Only you know whether making contact is the right course of action - you don't have to take the advice of well-meaning friends or relatives.*
- *Deep down, you'll know whether your relationship is meant to be. Spend time in stillness and silence and you'll be able to access this guidance.*

If Your Relationship Doesn't Rekindle

"Remember that sometimes not getting what you
want is a wonderful stroke of luck."
- Dalai Lama

What if it becomes clear that a reconciliation is never going to happen?

Remember that the end of a relationship doesn't mean you've lost love. Your capacity to love and be loved is always intact. When we reverse the flow of love from *getting* to *giving,* our desperate *need* to be loved falls away. Practice this outward flow of love and you cannot help but attract love.

If you still have an intense longing for your partner, you're probably mistaking the physical and sexual aspects of a relationship for happiness. While intensely enjoyable, these aspects bring temporary pleasure *only* and not lasting happiness. Always remember, a relationship won't bring you lasting happiness, unless you're *already* happy.

I'm not suggesting you resign yourself to a life of celibacy. Just know that you can be perfectly content without these physical pleasures until your next relationship materialises. Intense yearnings will pass as you work on your inner state.

The end of a relationship can bring huge positive transformation. This was certainly my experience after my big break up with Michael, the father of my son. This seemingly disastrous event turned out to be a blessing in disguise - one that catapulted me towards the much happier life I have now.

You, too, may one day look back on your break up in this way. Intense pain can trigger a series of events which would never have occurred had things remained as they were.

Until you learn the fundamental lesson that happiness must come from within, rather than from outer circumstances, suffering tends to keep repeating, often with increasing intensity. Eventually, it'll crack you open to reveal the happiness that was always there below the surface, waiting to be uncovered. Seeking happiness in outer conditions is a dead-end. However, sometimes we need to hit that dead-end repeatedly before we wake up.

If your relationship doesn't rekindle and you continue practicing the techniques we've covered, there are many rewards in store for you.

Long Term Consequences of Cleaning Up Your Inner World

Here are some side effects of doing the inner work:

- **You'll Become a More Authentic Version of Yourself**

    When I was deeply depressed, I always sensed there was a better version of 'me' - I just couldn't seem to access this person. I knew the real 'me' wasn't crippled with shyness, depression or an eating disorder. I knew I had creative abilities I wasn't expressing, and I knew I had much greater potential for health, happiness and success.

    As my mind quietened and I dropped my old mental baggage, a more sociable, energetic, loving and confident person emerged, quite effortlessly. Problems fell away and creative urges flowed through me. It had been my persistent and repetitive negative thinking which had been blocking this happier version of me, rather than any obstacles in my outer reality.

    This is in store for anyone who continues on this path. You may even have an Eckhart Tolle 'awakening'. Although very rare, there are people all over the world who experience a sudden shift in awareness as they separate from their thoughts. For most of us, though, this is a gradual unfolding rather than overnight enlightenment.

- **You'll Become More Resilient**

    With a quiet mind, you'll develop a great resilience to the ups and downs of life - a break up will feel like a ripple on a pond, rather than a storm in an ocean. Situations which might have distressed you previously, will affect you much less.

- **You'll Care Less About What Happens 'Out There'**

    As you become more content, you'll be much less attached to your outer circumstances because you're *already* feeling so good on the inside.

Anything good that happens will be a bonus, but your happiness won't depend on it. Seeking happiness on the outside will fall away. This is when the *real* magic starts to happen. Things you used to want desperately, often start showing up when you achieve this wonderful detached state.

- ## Other Areas of Your Life Will Improve

Not only is your romantic life likely to improve, but also your career, finances, health and family relationships. Goals you'd set years ago and forgotten about may start to materialize, out of the blue, in response to your new frequency.

During the year that it took to write this book, I experienced a whole series of unexpected but pleasing events. These were things I'd wanted for years but had largely forgotten about. I believe this happened because writing about the techniques here, made me practice them with much greater intensity than usual, and this took me to a new level of joy.

These effortless manifestations included several financial windfalls, free tennis lessons, a new garden fence funded by my neighbour, renewed contact with a cousin, two new friendships, the gift of a guitar, free tickets to see a favourite musician and several trips abroad to places I'd always wanted to visit.

These were not things I *desperately* wanted or needed and that's precisely what allowed them to flow so easily into my life. They were simply pleasurable side-effects of my very contented inner state.

Watch out for these spontaneous occurrences, even if they seem trivial. *Everything* is a 'manifestation' - big and small. It's easy to forget that these have arisen in response to your improved emotional state, so remember to make this important connection.

If you write these occurrences down and review them in a year's time, you may be astonished at how many good things have happened.

- **You May Not Want to Reunite With Your Partner**

The 'like attracts like' principle ensures we attract a partner who is on our emotional wavelength. This means that if you significantly alter your inner state, you may no longer be in resonance with your partner. You may stop longing to be with them, even if this seems inconceivable to you at the moment.

If you *do* reunite with your partner, unless they change with you, you may end up being the one who seeks to leave the relationship.

- **You May Find a More Compatible Partner**

It's best to recover fully from a break up *before* starting a new relationship. Rebound relationships are often unsuccessful because they're initiated from a place of unhappiness and lack.

Develop your own happiness *first* and you'll be in tune with a healthier relationship. When I cleaned up my inner state, I attracted a much happier and more compatible partner than any of my previous ones.

- **Things May Appear to Fall Apart**

> *"Sometimes good things fall apart so*
> *better things can fall together"*
> - Marilyn Monroe

As you change internally, your outer circumstances may shift and change unexpectedly. These changes may cause fear and discomfort. It may even look like your life is falling apart - the loss of a job or a friendship, for example. On some level, you probably wanted these changes to occur but the way it happens isn't always planned or expected.

If your life is to move from where you are now, to where you want it to be, some kind of change or loss is inevitable. The intelligent forces of nature will rearrange your circumstances so that they come into resonance with your new inner state.

The secret is not to panic or resist these changes but to realise it's all unfolding perfectly. As one door closes, another door opens.

Final Words

"If you accept all moments with a deep gratitude,
nothing ever goes wrong"
- Osho

In essence, this book is about rekindling love within you. When you tune to a more loving frequency, the right person - *whoever that may be* - will find you. There will be no forcing or trying involved.

The only real work you must do is to nurture a relaxed, peaceful and loving inner state. This involves letting go of problems and negative thoughts on a continuous daily basis, and no longer trying to fix your outer circumstances from a place of lack.

How you feel - moment by moment - must become the *most* important thing in your life, *rather* than taking outer action to feel better.

With practice, you'll become skilled at dropping fearful and anxious thoughts, as they arise, and withdrawing your attention from outer conditions which upset you. Make this your highest priority above all else and, perhaps for the first time, your life will become joyful and easy and as it should be.

If you're experiencing a lack of love, this lack will persist until you significantly reduce your thoughts and feelings of lack, and learn to broadcast from a more loving frequency.

Simply relaxing and letting go of problems is often all that's required to produce positive physical manifestations. However, remember that any improvements in your outer circumstances will bring you temporary pleasure only. They are not essential for happiness, because happiness is your natural state and you need nothing to be happy.

It took me a great deal of conscious awareness to drop my deeply ingrained stress-struggle approach to life. I'd spent so many years in 'fight or flight' mode, high on caffeine and sugar, forcing myself upstream, that it took time to unlearn this habit. I thought I needed to be in this high-stress state to achieve anything. In fact, I was rather proud of my extreme work ethic.

However, all I was achieving was depression, exhaustion, anxiety and an endless series of problems in my outer circumstances.

It's when we're in this high-stress state that obstacles seem to crop up continuously - gadgets malfunction, we have niggling health issues, we lose our keys, stub our toe, miss the train, spill the milk and so on and so forth. Then there are the larger scale problems that develop, such as relationship and financial difficulties.

If this sounds familiar to you, it's a sign that you need to tune to a more relaxed and peaceful frequency. Only when you change your inner state can you access a new outer reality.

When I slowed my life right down, it was like unblocking a pipe. The love, wealth and health that I'd been chasing so desperately, started to flow into my life. In the spiritual world, this principle is sometimes called the 'Law of Least Effort' - this is about accomplishing so much more from a peaceful and relaxed state.

If you've been swimming upstream most of your life, it can be very frightening to take your hands off the steering wheel. You may fear that if you stop trying and controlling, the bills won't get paid, you'll never find love, and your life will fall apart. However, nothing could be further from the truth.

You are part of an intelligent system which will guide you at every step - *if* you 'Let Go and Let God'. If there's any sense of forcing as you go about your day, you're moving *against* the current and interfering with the natural flow.

Sadly, most people are unable to believe that life can really work like this. It's too counterintuitive and different to the back-to-front, stress-struggle, approach which dominates our culture. Schools don't teach about the fluidity of the material world and the effect our mind has upon it. This means the majority live their entire life from the conditioned mind, with all its limiting stories and beliefs, thereby missing out on the enormous joy that comes from this very relaxed way of living.

Unlearning the old paradigm requires commitment and practice and you're likely to encounter resistance at first. However, pain is a great catalyst. The greater your suffering the more discipline and determination you'll be able to put into this.

You don't have to do this perfectly or continuously. For me, it's still a work in progress but it's enjoyable and, at times, quite magical. I no longer recognize the depressed and tortured soul I used to be. My life is now so much smoother and more relaxed - joyful moments come often, there's more laughter, love and abundance, and things just seem to fall into place. Change your energy signature and you change your life.

So, watch your thoughts intensely, be careful where you place your attention, *feel* your feelings, focus always on what you *do* want, love unconditionally, spend time being, appreciate and celebrate, act 'as if', go with the flow, reinterpret often, live in the moment and, above all else, simply relax and let go. Practice and repeat this formula and watch your life and relationships transform.

This takes time to master but you've got the rest of your life to practice. I promise you, miracles *will* happen along the way. Love will find you and you won't ever have to seek it.

REFERENCES

1. Tressoldi P.E., Storm L., & Radin D., (2010) Extrasensory Perception and Quantum Models of Cognition. *NeuroQuantology*, 8(4), 581-87.

2. Myers D., Diener E., (1995) Who Is Happy? *Psychological Science,* 6, 10-19.

3. Brickman P., Coates D., Janoff-Bulman R.J., (1979) Lottery Winners and Accident Victims: Is Happiness Relative? *Journal of Personality and Social Psychology,* 36, 917-27.

4. Lally P., Van Jaarsveld C., Potts H., Wardle J., (2010) How Are Habits Formed: Modelling Habit Formation in the Real World. *European Journal of Social Psychology,* 40, 998-1009.

ABOUT THE AUTHOR

Originally from Scotland, Louisa Jackson now lives in London with her partner, son and two dogs. She has an Honours and Masters degree in Psychology and a passion for all things scientific and psychological. As well as writing non-fiction, she writes and illustrates children's books. This book has been written under a pseudonym to protect the privacy of those mentioned.

Printed in Great Britain
by Amazon

66483868R00071